GLADIATOR vs CR.42 *FALCO*

1940–41

HÅKAN GUSTAVSSON AND
LUDOVICO SLONGO

First published in Great Britain in 2012 by Osprey Publishing, Midland House, West Way, Botley, Oxford OX2 0PH, UK

44-02 23rd Street, Suite 219, Long Island City, NY 11101, USA

E-mail: info@ospreypublishing.com

A CIP catalogue record for this book is available from the British Library

ISBN: 978 1 84908 708 7
PDF e-book ISBN: 978 1 84908 709 4
e-Pub ISBN: 978 1 78200 329 8

Edited by Tony Holmes and Phil Jarrett
Cover artworks and battlescene by Gareth Hector
Three-views, cockpits, gunsight and armament scrap views by Jim Laurier
Index by Alan Thatcher
Originated by PDQ Digital Media Solutions, UK
Printed in China through Bookbuilders

12 13 14 15 16   10 9 8 7 6 5 4 3 2 1

Osprey Publishing is supporting the Woodland Trust, the UK's leading woodland conservation charity, by funding the dedication of trees.

www.ospreypublishing.com

Acknowledgements

The authors would first like to thank their wives, Lotta and Eva, for their continuing support. This book is the result of many years of research, and the authors would like to thank the following individuals for help, inspiration and encouragement during this work – Stefano Lazzaro, Michele Maria Gaetani, Börje Henningsson, Roberto Gentilli, Tinus le Roux, Andrew Thomas, Guido Abate, Giorgio Apostolo, Rossella Baron, Nick Beale, Christer Bergström, Maria Teresa Bobba, Gianandrea Bussi, Enrico Cernuschi, Alide Comba, Fulvio Chianese, Brian Cull, Ferdinando D'Amico, Luca Delle Canne, Bruno Dilecce, Eugenio Eusebi, Alessandro Gazzi, Enrico Locatelli, Giovanni Massimello, Patricia Molloy, Enrico Neami, Michele Palermo, Manlio Palmieri, Roberto Pavan, Renato Zavattini and Csaba B. Stenge.

Gladiator cover art

At 0845 hrs on 28 November 1940 a formation of ten Fiat CR.42s of 150° *Gruppo*, equally drawn from 364ª and 365ª *Squadriglie*, took off from the port town of Vlorë, in Albania, for a patrol over the front. The Italian fighters were led by the unit's CO, Capitano Giorgio Graffer. At 1000 hrs, a formation of three Gloster Gladiators was discovered at 3,000m (10,000ft) between the towns of Konispol and Butrint, in Albania, and immediately attacked. 'A' Flight of No. 80 Sqn was in fact carrying out a patrol over the same area, with nine Gladiators divided into three vics of three. The vics were spaced three miles apart, and when the first was attacked by the Fiats the other two, which were not in view, were able to join combat, with deadly results, ten kilometres southwest of Delvinaki. After a hard dogfight, three Fiats were shot down and two pilots killed, one of whom was Graffer, while a fourth CR.42 was damaged and its pilot wounded. Four Gladiators were shot up, one of them badly, and its pilot, Flt Lt E. G. 'Tap' Jones, was wounded. A fifth failed to return after Flg Off H. U. Sykes collided with the CR.42 of Sergente Corrado Mignani, both pilots losing their lives. (Artwork by Gareth Hector)

CR.42 cover art

At around 0800 hrs on 13 December 1940, a patrol of six Gladiators from No. 3 Sqn RAAF and a formation of ten CR.42s of 9° *Gruppo* clashed over an area between the Egyptian coastal town of Sollum and the nearby Halfaya Pass. The combat started at medium altitude when the Australian pilots discovered a vic of five SM.79s of 33° *Gruppo* and dived on the bombers in line astern. Unbeknown to them, the SM.79s were being escorted by the CR.42s, which, in turn, bounced the Gladiators and shot five of them down in just a matter of a minutes. At the very beginning of the combat the leader of the Italian formation, Capitano Antonio Larsimont Pergameni, closed too rapidly on his target – the aircraft of Flg Off Wilfred Arthur – and ran into it from dead astern. The Gladiator's wings folded up and the fighter fell like a stone. Although his CR.42 was badly damaged, Larsimont was able to regain control and land at Menastir airfield, where the aircraft subsequently had to be abandoned. (Artwork by Gareth Hector)

CONTENTS

INTRODUCTION

When Italy entered World War II on 10 June 1940, its main opponent was Great Britain and the Commonwealth (the war against France only lasted two weeks). The battlefield for these two opposing forces was predominantly the Mediterranean, with a particular focus on North Africa, Malta and Greece. Fighting also took place further afield in East Africa.

Italy was not well prepared for this war, and its entry into it seems to have been mostly an opportunistic gamble by the nation's leader, Benito Mussolini, who longed for a share in the spoils of war. Although its armed forces struggled valiantly, Italy was to suffer humiliating defeats during the autumn and winter of 1940 until the intervention of German forces, which turned the Allied tide of victory until the autumn of 1942.

For the British, the Mediterranean was a secondary front. The key objective for Allied forces in-theatre was to keep the Suez Canal open to allow vessels to travel between the homeland and India. However, it became more important after the immediate threat of invasion of Britain had diminished in the winter of 1940-41, being the only theatre where Allied forces could meet their opponents on the ground. Much propaganda was initially generated following the exploits of British and Commonwealth troops on the battlefields of North Africa in particular, and this duly resulted in British strengths being routinely overrated, while those of its Italian opponents were underrated.

On these battlefields, the last, and arguably the best, biplane fighters clashed – Italy's Fiat CR.42 and Britain's Gloster Gladiator. The respective types' deployment on these fronts was of slightly different origin. Drawing upon experience during the Spanish Civil War, the Italians (and also the Soviet Union) still believed that there was a place in a modern war for the biplane fighter, complemented by monoplanes, while

Britain had progressively transferred its Gladiators to secondary fronts, re-equipping its fighter units on the Channel Front with modern Hawker Hurricanes and Supermarine Spitfires. Thus, these two outdated biplanes formed the major equipment of the fighter forces in the Mediterranean area for the first months of the war.

The authors have spent many years researching the participating air forces in these battlefields, with the aim of overcoming all British and Italian propaganda in order to be able to produce an unbiased account of what really happened, and provide a fair description for both of the sides involved.

CHRONOLOGY

1934

12 September First flight of the SS.37 Gloster Gladiator prototype.

1935

3 April Gladiator prototype taken on charge by the Air Ministry and given the military serial K5200.

1937

16 February The first Gladiator I, K6129, is taken on RAF charge.

22 February The first Gladiators, K6130-K6137, enter service with No. 72 Sqn at Tangmere.

1938

24 February First known victory credited to a Gladiator when four Chinese examples share in the destruction of an Imperial Japanese Navy Nakajima E8N 'Dave' reconnaissance floatplane.

23 May First flight of the Fiat CR.42.

September During the Munich Crisis the RAF's frontline strength includes five Gladiator squadrons.

1939

Spring The first CR.42s are delivered to the *Regia Aeronautica*. The first unit to be allocated the type is 53° *Stormo* C.T.

3 September Great Britain and France declare war on Germany and World War II begins. At this time there are still four Gladiator squadrons within Fighter Command in the UK.

1940

10 May The first aerial victory for the CR.42 is claimed by a Belgian example over a German Junkers Ju 52/3m.

10 June Italy enters World War II by declaring war on Britain and France.

14 June First combat between RAF and *Regia Aeronautica* fighters. CR.42s of 90ª *Squadriglia* claim a Gladiator destroyed, although none were actually lost.

19 June Gladiator pilots (from No. 33 Sqn) make their first claims for victories over the CR.42 when they engage fighters from 10° *Gruppo* C.T., which loses two aircraft. A single Gladiator is shot down in return.

Gladiator Is of No. 72 Sqn undergo maintenance in a hangar at Church Fenton in the summer of 1937. The aircraft closest to the camera has a Fairey-Reed type three-bladed metal propeller. (Rennie Cafley)

An overturned CR.42 of 365ª *Squadriglia*, 150° *Gruppo*, probably after an accident suffered in Greece by Sergente Domenico Facchini on 13 November 1940. (Roberto Gentilli)

1941

29 May
CR.42 pilots claim their final successes over the Gladiator when three aircraft of *'Squadriglia Speciale Iraq'* are credited with two victories and one probable over Al Habbaniyah, Iraq.

24 October
Last known claim in combat between Gladiators and CR.42s, when a pilot of No. 3 Sqn, South African Air Force, is credited with the destruction of a Fiat fighter in the Ambazzo area of East Africa.

1943

15 February
Last known Gladiator claim, when a Finnish example from LeLv 16 downs a Soviet R-5 over Kärkijärvi.

1945

8 February
Possibly the last claim made by a CR.42 when aircraft from the Luftwaffe's *Nachtschlachtgruppe* 7 are involved in combat with P-38 Lightnings of the 14th Fighter Group (FG) over Croatia. Three CR.42LWs fell to the USAAF fighters, but a P-38 is also claimed by an unknown German pilot. The 14th FG lost two Lightnings during this mission.

Two burnt out Gladiators destroyed on the ground in Greece, possibly at Paramythia, in early 1941. (Roberto Gentilli)

DESIGN AND DEVELOPMENT

GLOSTER GLADIATOR

As the last biplane fighter to enter RAF service, the Gloster Gladiator marked the end of an era. It is worth noting that it was put into service after the Hurricane and Spitfire had been ordered into mass production.

In 1930 the Air Ministry issued Specification F.7/30, calling for a replacement for the Bristol Bulldog. The specification called for a maximum speed of 250mph, an armament of not less than four forward-firing machine guns and such ease of handling as to enable the fighter to be operated both by day- and nightfighter squadrons. The specification also required the use of the Rolls-Royce Goshawk engine. Designs were submitted by Hawker, Fairey, Bristol, Westland, Vickers and Supermarine (with its original inverted-gull-wing Spitfire). None of these proposals was found to be satisfactory. Although the Gloster Aircraft Company did not submit a design, further orders were placed for its Gauntlet fighter due to the inability of the British aviation industry to provide the RAF with a satisfactory design to replace it.

The advent, as yet only on paper, of the Spitfire and Hurricane monoplane fighters threatened to eliminate the F.7/30 requirement altogether. It was only when it seemed that a gap might occur in defence requirements between the biplane fighter's demise and Service acceptance of the monoplanes that Gloster realised that a development of

the Gauntlet might well meet the F.7/30 requirements and win worthwhile production contracts. The company began construction of a prototype (the SS.37) in the early spring of 1934 and completed it in September of that year, when it made its maiden flight in the hands of Flt Lt P. E. G. Sayer. Powered by a 645hp Bristol Mercury VIS radial engine and armed with two Vickers and two drum-fed Lewis machine guns, the prototype achieved a speed of 242mph at 11,500ft.

The Air Ministry sponsored protracted evaluation trials, and transferred the prototype to RAF charge as K5200 on 3 April 1935. In June of that year production plans were put forward, frontline aircraft being fitted with the 840hp Mercury IX engine, four Vickers Mk V guns (pending the delivery of Browning 0.303-in guns from BSA) and improved wheel discs. Within two weeks of the plans being unveiled, production specification F.14/35 had been drawn up and agreed and a contract for 23 aircraft awarded to Gloster as a result of the RAF's Expansion Programme.

The Bristol Mercury VIIIA (or later the Mercury IX) engine was a shorter-stroke 1935 development of the renowned Jupiter. A single-row nine-cylinder engine, it produced 840hp for takeoff from sea level up to 1,000ft and had a maximum continuous climbing rate of 700-730hp at sea level and 795-825hp at 13,000ft. Its continuous cruising power was 685hp at 13,000 ft, and maximum (all-out) power for five minutes was 840hp at 14,000ft. The Mercury was fairly light (1,065lb) but rather cumbersome (frontal area $14.7ft^2$), and its major weakness was that it drove low-efficiency fixed-pitch Watts wooden two-blade or Fairey Reed metal three-blade propellers.

On 1 July 1935 the name Gladiator was officially announced for the fighter. The prototype, K5200, underwent numerous trials, which resulted in the addition of a sliding cockpit canopy for the pilot. Production soon got underway at Hucclecote, with construction of the whole batch being undertaken simultaneously so that the entire order was completed almost at the same time. The first aircraft, K6129, was

A line-up of Gladiator Is, with K6143 nearest the camera, at the Gloster Aircraft Company factory before delivery to No. 72 Sqn. This photograph was probably taken in early February 1937, as K6143 was delivered to the unit on the 12th of that month. It was subsequently sent to No. 112 Sqn when this unit formed on 11 May 1939, and was then shipped to North Africa. Later, K6143 served with 'K' Flight and No. 117 Sqn. On 20 June 1941 a tyre burst on landing at Khartoum and the aircraft swung and was damaged beyond repair. (Vincent Jones)

GLADIATOR I

27ft 5in

11ft 9in

32ft 3in

taken on RAF charge on 16 February 1937 and the last, K6151, on 4 March that year. A second batch of 186 Gladiators was ordered, starting with K7892, and these were delivered between April and November 1937, the last being K8055. Only 164 of the 186 were built, however, K8056 to K8077 being cancelled. A further batch of 16 Mk Is, L7608 to L7622, was delivered between December 1937 and January 1938.

The first unit to receive Gladiators was No. 72 Sqn at Tangmere in February 1937. Following further deliveries to the unit, No. 3 Sqn at Kenley received most of the remainder of the first production batch in March/April.

Thus far, all aircraft had been delivered with Lewis guns under the lower wings, pending clearance of the Vickers Mk V guns remote from the pilot. Although clearance was eventually achieved, Service units encountered such difficulties with these guns that the Vickers weapons were seldom used. With the arrival of the Browning (Colt licence) gun, reversion to the Vickers V, Vickers 'K' and Lewis was favoured only in dire emergencies.

The first unit to equip with Browning-armed Gladiators (from the second batch) was No. 54 Sqn at Hornchurch on 27 April, followed shortly thereafter by No. 74 Sqn, also at Hornchurch. However, the Gladiators on the latter unit were soon passed on to No. 3 Sqn, their place being taken almost immediately by Gauntlets. Next in line for the new fighter was No. 80 Sqn at Henlow, in May 1937, but within a year this unit had moved to the Middle East. Other units to receive Gladiators in 1937 were Nos. 65, 73, 87 and 56 Sqns.

The fighter's introduction into RAF service was surprisingly difficult. Although pilots were happy with the Gladiator, the accident rate was so high (albeit mostly comprising mishaps of a superficial nature) during operational training that a small replacement batch of 28 Mk IIs (L8005-L8032) was hurriedly built. As it transpired, these aircraft were delivered into storage in September 1938, where they remained until they were shipped to the Middle East the following year.

Most accidents were caused by pilots being caught out by the fighter's increased wing loading. Many aviators also lacked experience in landing aircraft that boasted such generous flap area. As a result of the latter feature, the new biplane stalled more abruptly. With an increased tendency to drop a wing, Gladiators suffered from 'a plague' of damaged wingtips. The Gloster fighter also proved to be relatively easy to flat spin, and great care was needed when recovering from such a manoeuvre. Spinning at night was forbidden.

Notwithstanding these handling foibles, in the long run the Gladiator proved to be a valuable stepping stone for future Spitfire and Hurricane pilots, who gained experience with sliding canopies and landing flaps. Significantly, records show that pilots on monoplane fighter squadrons who had previously flown Gladiators suffered far fewer accidents than those who had come straight from Gauntlets.

By September 1937 all eight Gladiator squadrons had reached operational status. The following year saw a shift in emphasis from the Gladiator to the Hurricane. It was now public policy that for every squadron equipped with Gladiators, another would be re-equipped with Hurricanes or Spitfires. In place of Nos. 3 and 56 Sqns, who relinquished their biplane fighters for Hurricanes early in the year, Nos. 25 and 85 Sqns took on full establishments of Gladiators. In place of Nos. 73 and 87 Sqns came the first of the Auxiliary Air Force units, No. 607 'County of Durham' Sqn, based at Usworth. Moreover, realising that should war come to Europe Britain's overseas trade routes would be critically vulnerable, the RAF started despatching Gladiator squadrons to the Middle East for the defence of the Suez Canal.

Thus, at the time of Neville Chamberlain's much criticised peace overtures, which culminated in the Munich appeasement, the defence of Britain rested upon a fighter force that predominantly consisted of biplanes in 19 frontline and six auxiliary squadrons. So, with the knowledge that Britain needed a minimum of 52 fighter squadrons to repel potential invaders, military planners now had clear information as to the size of the expansion that lay ahead. So great was their task that, when war finally arrived a year later, the Gladiator had by no means disappeared from the scene.

At the outbreak of war in September 1939 the home defence of Great Britain rested upon Hurricanes, Spitfires and, to a lesser extent, Bristol Blenheims and Gladiators.

Two Gladiator squadrons (Nos. 607 and 615) took part in the French campaign of 1939-40 as part of the British Expeditionary Force. Their pilots made some interceptions and lodged some claims against the Luftwaffe during the winter, but the squadrons were in the process of re-equipping with Hurricanes when the Germans attacked on 10 May 1940. There were no known claims made by Gladiator pilots during this period as a result.

The only major combat seen by the Gladiator on the home front came during the two expeditions to Norway between April and June 1940, when the pilots of No. 263 Sqn performed well against the Luftwaffe. They claimed around 35 enemy aircraft destroyed or damaged, but suffered significant losses in return. The squadron was annihilated as an operational unit with the sinking of the aircraft carrier HMS *Glorious* on 8 June during the retreat from Norway.

FIAT CR.42

The Fiat CR.42 *Falco* resulted from the Italian belief that there was still a role for the highly manoeuvrable biplane fighter. This belief had been strengthened by the achievements of biplane fighters in Spain since 1936, especially the Fiat CR.32. The CR.42 was derived from this earlier type, retaining its unequal-wingspan configuration, and the experimental CR.40 and CR.41 fighters, which had introduced a radial engine.

In July 1935 the Italian Air Ministry issued a specification for a new fighter. In response, Fiat's veteran chief designer Ingegner Celestino Rosatelli developed a biplane, seeking to exploit to the full the possibilities of the new Fiat A74 engine that was then still at the development stage.

Both the engine and propeller of the Fiat fighter were of American origin. The two-row, 14-cylinder Fiat A74 R1C38 was a 1935 derivative of the famous Pratt & Whitney Twin Wasp engine. Apart from the longer stroke of the Fiat, the main difference was the crankshaft, which was of Italian design. A compact engine (frontal area 12.2ft²), the A74 R1C38 weighed 1,312lbs dry. More conservatively rated than its American ancestor, it developed 860-900 (metric) hp for takeoff at sea level, 740hp at sea level,

840hp at 12,467ft, 840hp at 14,108ft and 960hp at 9,843ft (war emergency power for a few minutes). Heavier but more streamlined than the Gladiator's Mercury, it was geared to a three-blade variable-pitch constant-speed Fiat-Hamilton propeller, which made much more efficient use of the engine's power than the Mercury's fixed-pitch propeller.

The fighter's basic design was changed several times in the space of a few months, particularly with regard to its armament, which progressed from one 20mm cannon and one 12.7mm weapon to three 12.7mm guns, then three 12.7mm weapons and one 7.7mm gun and, finally, two 12.7mm guns only.

In 1936, after a series of inspections, the project was accepted by the Air Ministry and construction of a prototype was ordered. Work started at Aeritalia in 1937, but because the factory was overloaded with the production and development of the Fiat CR.32 and BR.20, it was not until May 1938 that the prototype (NC 1) was completed. The CR.42 made its maiden flight on 23 May 1938, piloted by Comandante Valentino Cus. Flight-testing started

A CR.42 of 73ª *Squadriglia*, 9° *Gruppo* has maintenance performed on its two-row, 14-cylinder Fiat A74 R1C38 engine at El Adem in 1940. Sand ingestion caused innumerable problems for the CR.42 in the early months of the war in North Africa. Note the *squadriglia's* red flash insignia painted onto the fighter's wheel spat. (Roberto Gentilli)

immediately, and NC 1 often completed three or four tests in a single day, changing hands continually between the pilot and technicians, who carried out modifications and improvements.

In the summer of 1938 Fiat, and the CR.42, received numerous delegations from abroad – Hungarian, Portuguese, Bulgarian, Japanese, Bolivian, Spanish, Finnish, Swedish, Iranian, Thai and Brazilian parties all inspected the aircraft, sometimes arranging for test flights by their own pilots. Interest in the CR.42 was further stimulated by the success of the CR.32 in Spain. A number of air staffs were thus led to believe that the CR.42, combining flight characteristics similar to the CR.32 with a performance not too far removed from that of the monoplane fighters of the time, would turn out to be an excellent machine for air combat.

On 16 February 1938 the Italian Air Ministry ordered a first batch of 200 machines. In addition, an agreement was reached with the Hungarian government for the supply

CR.42

27ft 1.76in

11ft 9.33in

32ft 9.88in

This CR.42, probably from 413ᵃ *Squadriglia*, was captured by South African forces at Addis Ababa, in Abyssinia, in April 1941. In the background is a Lockheed Lodestar. (Roberto Gentilli)

OPPOSITE
CR.42 MM6271 of 412ᵃ *Squadriglia*, at Asmara in January 1941, was flown by Capitano Mario Visintini. It wore the standard three-tone camouflage of Verde Mimetico 3 and Marrone Mimetico 2 mottles over a Giallo Mimetico 3 base. Like all the fighters within the unit, it had neither an individual number nor a *squadriglia* number, but the fuselage bore a red prancing horse over a black silhouette of Africa. Although this was originally conceived as a unit insignia, at this stage of the war the badge was possibly carried only by Visintini's aeroplane, so it thus resembled a personal insignia. This machine was also equipped with a ring-and-bead gunsight and a radio receiver.

of 20 aircraft, with delivery starting from mid-1939. Subsequently, following further orders, the total delivered reached 50 machines.

In the spring of 1939 the first aircraft of the first batch of 200 (MM4265-MM4464) for the *Regia Aeronautica* were completed. Compared with the prototype, the differences were minimal. The tailwheel was fixed and no longer retractable, the engine cowling and the air intake of the oil radiator had been partly redesigned, two instruments had been added to the panel and the gunsight was of the reflector type (San Giorgio Tipo B), and no longer telescopic.

The first unit to be allocated CR.42s was 53° *Stormo* C.T. at Caselle (Turin), followed by 1° *Stormo* at Campoformido and 3° *Stormo* at Mirafiori (Turin). The pilots of 367ᵃ *Squadriglia* (151° *Gruppo*, 53° *Stormo*) took advantage of the new machine's excellent flying characteristics and established an aerobatic team of five aircraft. The idea was that their repertoire should not be limited to classic manoeuvres, but should also include high speed aerobatics. The debut of the new formation, led by Capitano Simeone Marsan, took place on 15 May 1939 during Mussolini's visit to Turin. The routine was well received, with the fighters' high-speed passes at the height of the grandstand being particularly memorable according to those that witnessed the event!

TECHNICAL SPECIFICATIONS

GLADIATOR I

Production Gladiators had an enclosed cockpit and also differed from the prototype in being fitted with a later type of Bristol Mercury engine, the Mercury IX. The fuselage-mounted Vickers Mk III machine guns were prone to jamming, and were replaced by Browning 0.303-in weapons. However, until substantial numbers of these guns could be produced, the first production Gladiators retained their underwing Lewis machine guns until they were replaced by Brownings. The Gladiator I was delivered to the RAF in four batches totalling 230 aircraft.

GLADIATOR II

Later Gladiators (from N2265) were of the Mk II type, with the Mercury VIIIA engine and numerous detail changes, including modified instrumentation. Some late-standard Mk Is were converted to Mk IIs by alteration of the powerplant and other minor modifications. The Gladiator II was delivered to the RAF in seven batches totalling 250 aircraft.

Gladiators of No. 1 Sqn SAAF, probably at Khartoum in August 1940. Note the absence of wheel hub covers on some machines, revealing their Dowty internally sprung wheels. (SAAF Museum)

A No. 1 Sqn SAAF Gladiator is refuelled by hand in the field using flimsy tins that have been delivered in the back of a truck. (SAAF Museum)

SEA GLADIATOR

The Sea Gladiator was powered by the Bristol Mercury VIII. Some earlier Gladiator IIs (N2265-N2302) were converted to Sea Gladiator (Interim) standard through the addition of a 'V' deck arrester hook, a naval TR 9 radio and recalibration of the instruments to register knots. Later aircraft, starting with N5500, were built as Sea Gladiators from the outset and had two additional Browning guns fitted to the upper wing (it is not known if these guns were ever fitted to Service aircraft, however). The Sea Gladiator also had provision for a dinghy in a fairing between the undercarriage legs. The Sea Gladiator (including the Interim version) was delivered in three batches totalling 98 aircraft.

FIAT CR.42

Although some 1,600 CR.42s were delivered to the *Regia Aeronautica*, there were no significant production variants apart from two specific modifications. Thus, the standard CR.42s, built in 14 main batches, remained virtually identical to the prototype. The main changes from an operational point of view consisted of upgrading the instrumentation and, belatedly, fitting a two-way radio.

The first modification (from the start of 1941) comprised the fitting of underwing bomb racks of up to 100kg capacity for ground-attack missions which, together with the adoption of engine and accessory sand filters, produced a variant intended for service in North Africa known as the AS (*Africa Settentrionale*).

GLADIATOR GUNS

The Gladiator was fitted with four Browning 0.303-in. machine guns. Two were sited on either side of the forward fuselage, firing through the propeller arc by means of an interrupter gear. There was a 600-round belt box for each gun. The other two guns were fitted in fairings beneath the lower wings, with a 400-round belt box each. The Browning was often criticised for not having enough punch to shoot down contemporary enemy fighters and bombers, but in combat against the unarmoured CR.42 it was an effective weapon.

Another modification was the fitting of an auxiliary fuel tank in the fuselage, and several dozen machines destined for the eastern Mediterranean were designated *EGEO* ('Aegean version') following this change. Improved instrumentation and longer flame-damping exhausts produced the CN (*Caccia notturna*), employed with little success as a nightfighter.

Several CR.42s had one or both of their 12.7mm guns replaced by the lighter 7.7mm equivalents mostly at unit level, but also by maintenance depots or at the factory. This reduced the aircraft's empty weight and allowed more fuel to be carried. These variants were not given any specific designation.

The last CR.42 variant to fly with the Italian Air Force was the two-seat CR.42B, a prototype of which had been built by the Agusta company in 1943. Production was

A trio CR.42s from 78ª *Squadriglia*, 13° *Gruppo*, probably at El Adem in 1940. From the mid-1930s the basic formation of the *Regia Aeronautica* was the Pattuglia of three aeroplanes, which could fly in line astern, line abreast, echelon or, more often, in a vic. (Roberto Gentilli)

CR.42 GUNS

The CR.42 was designed to be fitted with two Breda SAFAT 12.7mm machine guns with 400 rounds each, mounted on top of the forward fuselage and firing through the propeller arc. In fact in many aeroplanes serving at the beginning of the conflict, such as the one depicted here, one of the 12.7mm weapons was replaced by a smaller Breda SAFAT 7.7mm gun. The 12.7mm weapon was heavy, bulky and had a low rate-of-fire that was worsened by the synchronisation system and a low muzzle velocity. Consequently, the gun was not very well suited to coping with a nimble target like the Gladiator.

Probably seen at Palermo airfield in 1941, this CR.42 and its proud pilot were assigned to 80ª *Squadriglia, 17° Gruppo*. (Roberto Gentilli)

undertaken only after the war, however, several single-seaters being modified with a considerable fuselage stretch, an additional rear cockpit and a lengthened engine mounting to maintain the correct centre of gravity. CR.42 two-seaters remained in service until about 1950.

Gladiator I and CR.42 comparison specifications		
	Gladiator I	CR.42
Powerplant	840hp	860-900hp
	Bristol Mercury IX	Fiat A 74 RC38
Dimensions		
Span	32ft 3in.	32ft 9.88in.
Length	27ft 5in.	27ft 1.67in.
Height	11ft 9in.	11ft 9.33in.
Wing area	323 sq ft	241.111 sq ft
Weights		
Empty	3,217lb	3,929lb
Loaded	4,592lb	5,059lb
Performance		
Max speed	253mph at 14,500ft	272mph at 17,300ft
Range	428 miles	573 miles
Rate of climb to 20,000ft	9.3 min	7.5 min
Service ceiling	32,800ft	33,136ft
Armament	4 x 0.303-in. Brownings	2 x 12.7mm SAFATs

THE STRATEGIC SITUATION

In June 1940 the RAF was heavily engaged against the Luftwaffe in France and Norway. The intervention of Italy in the conflict was seen as unavoidable, but there was very little to spare in terms of modern eight-gun monoplanes in the class of the Spitfire and the Hurricane to build up strength in sectors threatened by the Italians such as the Middle East and Mediterranean. All of the RAF fighter units stationed in those theatres flew Gladiators, production of which had ceased in 1939, and their use by British based units was just ending.

When, finally, Italy declared war on 10 June 1940, the Gladiator in its Mk I and Mk II versions equipped Nos. 33, 80 and 112 Sqns (the latter minus one flight) in Egypt. These squadrons had started to reach the sector in 1938 following the progressive worsening of relations with Italy. No. 94 Sqn had recently formed in Aden, and it was still lacking its full complement of fighters. Indeed, it had only one flight equipped with Gladiator IIs. No. 112 Sqn's 'B' Flight was in Sudan, while on Malta, a small fighter unit (christened the Hal Far Station Fighter Flight) had been formed during the spring of 1940 and equipped with a few Sea Gladiators left behind by the Fleet Air Arm (FAA).

Gladiator GK-Z of No. 80 Sqn in mid-1939. The unit had been in Egypt with its Gloster biplane fighters since April of the previous year. Note the squadron's bell emblem painted on the Gladiator's fin. (Andrew Thomas)

Gladiator I K8011/YK-S of No. 80 Sqn takes off in 1940 with future 11-victory ace Flg Off John Lapsley in the cockpit. Flg Off H. D. W. Flower claimed a probable CR.42 while flying this aircraft on 8 August 1940. K8011 was later passed on to the Royal Iraqi Air Force and was struck off charge on 21 June 1941. (Andrew Thomas)

Re-equipment of most of these units with Hurricanes was already scheduled, but a shortage of the Hawker monoplanes owing to the demands of Fighter Command units meant that, after a first batch of machines passed through France in late spring, the first regular deliveries to Middle East Command did not arrive until the end of September. The Gladiator would therefore be forced to remain in frontline service until the spring of 1941.

On paper, this force might look small compared with that of its opponent, but while it is true that RAF Middle East Command had to fight the whole *Regia Aeronautica*, it is worth pointing out that, owing to their status as detached units far from the UK, these squadrons had aircraft complements that were much larger than those of standard Fighter Command units, and larger than that of an Italian *Gruppo*. For example, No. 80 Sqn moved to Egypt with a first-line strength of 21 aeroplanes, plus 11 more airframes kept as reserves and ten available on a long-term basis. A fully equipped *Gruppo* could count on 36 fighters or, more frequently, only 27.

In greater detail, on 10 June 1940 the RAF fighter units in-theatre could list a total of 77 Gladiator Is and 57 Gladiator IIs in Egypt, part on charge with the three resident squadrons and part stored at Aboukir. Another 18 Mk IIs were to be loaned to the South African Air Force (SAAF), some 17 Sea Gladiators were kept in the FAA depot and 18 Mk IIs were reserved for No. 94 Sqn in Aden. On top of this, before the war the Royal Egyptian Air Force (REAF) had received 18 Mk Is and 18 Mk IIs, and these, although Egypt was to remain neutral, were from time to time repossessed by the RAF to replace its own losses. Therefore, at the beginning of the war RAF Middle East Command could muster 141 Gladiators and the 36 Egyptian machines in North Africa and ten Gladiator Is and 36 Mk IIs in East Africa. It was in fact a respectable force, roughly equivalent to that of its opponent.

Opposing them was the *Regia Aeronautica*, whose re-equipment programme, christened 'Programma R', was still ongoing when the Italians declared war. Conceived after the Abyssinian Campaign of 1935-36, the programme's aim was to establish ten *Stormi*, four *Gruppi* and six *Squadriglie* of fighters (a total of 971 aeroplanes) by July 1940, but it had been revised and accelerated in 1939 with the beginning of World War II. At that time the programme was lagging somewhat behind schedule, trying to complete the re-equipment of at least those units that it was possible to refurbish during the summer of 1940.

When the original programme had been devised it had been decided to equip four *Stormi* and three *Gruppi* with the CR.42. Apart from its manoeuvrability, this fighter had an inferior performance compared with the monoplane prototypes that had won the official competition for the new Italian interceptor aircraft in 1938, but to offset a possible failure of these types it was decided to put the *Falco* into production as an interim fighter. This choice, very often criticised, proved to be the right one when Italy entered the war in the summer of 1940, because the monoplanes were still far from reaching a sufficient level of operational readiness, and without the CR.42 the Italian fighter arm would have fought its initial battles using the thoroughly obsolete CR.32.

At the beginning of the conflict some 332 CR.42s equipped the *Squadriglie* of the *Regia Aeronautica*, of which 213 were combat ready. In northwestern Italy, forming the ranks of IIª *Divisione Aerea 'Borea'*, the units that comprised all the CR.42-equipped fighter groups of Iª *Squadra Aerea* ranged against France were 53° *Stormo* (150° and 151° *Gruppi*) and 3° *Stormo* (18° and 23° *Gruppi*). Additionally, in northeastern Italy, the IIª *Squadra Aerea*, which had moved to Sicily, had left behind 9° *Gruppo* of 4° *Stormo*, again flying CR.42s, to guard the frontier with Yugoslavia.

In Sicily, as part of Iª *Divisione Aerea 'Aquila'*, 157° *Gruppo* provided CR.42 fighters for IIª *Squadra Aerea* operating over the British fortress of Malta and against French forces in Tunisia. In Libya, as part of the *'Aeronautica della Libia'* (which was soon to became Vª *Squadra Aerea*) opposing British forces in Egypt, were CR.42-equipped 10° and 13° *Gruppi*. The former unit had flown into Libya from Gorizia on 12 June 1940, whilst the latter (which was part of 2° *Stormo*) had still to begin its conversion from CR.32s to CR.42s.

An additional unit, 160° *Gruppo Autonomo*, which was part of the *'Aeronautica dell'Albania'*, was equipped with a few of the new Fiat biplane fighters in Albania as part of the air force there.

Finally, the *Regia Aeronautica* had planned to send a complete *Gruppo* of CR.42s to reinforce the air force based in East Africa. In fact, during the spring of 1940 412ª

An overturned CR.42 of 91ª *Squadriglia*, 10° *Gruppo* in North Africa in 1940. (Roberto Gentilli)

CR.42 4-75 of 75ª *Squadriglia*, 23ª *Gruppo* over Sicily in the summer of 1940. (Maria Teresa Bobba)

Squadriglia, formed in December 1939 with pilots taken from 84ª *Squadriglia* of 4° *Stormo*, and 413ª, formed in the same period with pilots from 364ª *Squadriglia* of 53° *Stormo*, were sent by ship to Eritrea. A third squadron, 414ª *Squadriglia*, formed with resident personnel taken from disbanded units, was also to be equipped with CR.42s. The units protected the bases of Gura and Assab, with a detachment in Massawa in the north of the country, and faced Commonwealth forces based in Sudan and Aden.

Thus, at the beginning of the war, Italy confronted British and Commonwealth forces in the Mediterranean and on two main land fronts – North Africa and East Africa. Over each of these sectors the fighter forces were equipped almost exclusively with Fiat and Gloster biplanes.

MALTA

Over the Mediterranean, air operations were centred on the fortress island of Malta. Here, the Fiat fighters of 9° and later 23° and 17° *Gruppi* (the last-named unit changed from CR.32s to CR.42s because the planned Macchi C.200 monoplane fighters were not yet available) met the Gladiators of the Hal Far Fighter Flight (soon to become No. 261 Sqn) on a few occasions. The British unit soon re-equipped with Hurricane Is, and from the late summer of 1940 onwards the Gladiator had virtually disappeared. For the *Regia Aeronautica*, C.200s started appearing over the island with increasing frequency once the teething problems that still troubled them had been finally solved, the Macchis replacing the CR.42s in the ranks of 17° *Gruppo*. But it was not until the beginning of 1941 that the C.200 became the main Italian fighter in the sector, the CR.42 remaining in frontline daytime service in the ranks of 23° *Gruppo* until the very end of 1941.

NORTH AFRICA

In North Africa the first Hurricane unit, No. 274 Sqn, was formed in late August, and during the following months No. 33 Sqn was also equipped with the fighter, its first examples arriving by the Takoradi route. Meanwhile, No. 3 Sqn Royal Australian Air Force (RAAF) had reached North Africa too, where it was equipped with the Gladiators made available by the Hurricanes' arrival.

On the Italian side, the two *Gruppi* of 2° *Stormo* that were still partly or totally equipped with CR.32s in June moved to the CR.42 and were joined by 9° *Gruppo* from Sicily in July and by 151° *Gruppo* from northern Italy in September. Gladiators and Fiat fighters clashed many times from July to November, but with the start of the first Commonwealth offensive (Operation *Compass*) on 9 December 1940, operational use of the Gladiator – then still flying with the Australian unit and No. 112 Sqn – began to decrease until it ceased altogether on February 1941 with the arrival of the first Hurricanes for No. 3 Sqn RAAF. This was not the case for the CR.42 units, however, as although they were supplemented by some Fiat G.50-equipped squadrons from December 1940, they continued to hold the line until the spring of 1941. Surviving CR.42s were then assigned point-defence and convoy escort duties, before finally starting a second life as fighter-bombers from late 1941 until the El Alamein battles in October 1942.

TOP
Future ranking No. 112 Sqn Gladiator ace Flg Off Joe Fraser enjoys a cold beer after a forced landing in the North African desert. Behind him, a fitter from the unit is attempting to get to grips with the fighter's mechanical maladies. (Patricia Molloy)

BOTTOM
CR.42 394-3 of 394ª *Squadriglia*, 160° *Gruppo*, over Greece in 1941. On the fuselage side just forward of the cockpit can be seen a silhouette of Mussolini's head. This unofficial unit marking was adopted by 394ª *Squadriglia* during the Greek campaign. (Roberto Gentilli)

GREECE

In October 1940 a new front was opened when Italy declared war on Greece. The British quickly secured Crete and then sent an air expeditionary force to help the Greeks, whose air force was at risk of ceasing to operate due to the combined effect of operational attrition and a lack of spare parts. One of the first units to arrive from Egypt was No. 80 Sqn with 20 Gladiator IIs, its 'B' Flight landing in Athens on 18 November and 'A' Flight flying in the following day. Later, on 2 December, the RAF supplied the *Elliniki Vassiliki Aeroporia* with 13 or 14 Gladiators taken from No. 80 Sqn and the Storage Depot at Aboukir, and they equipped the 21 *Mira*, previously flying Polish-designed PZL P.24s. Finally, on 23 January 1941, No. 112 Sqn started to arrive in Greece. While No. 80 Sqn was re-equipped with Hurricanes in February, No. 112 Sqn soldiered on with its Gladiators until the fall of Crete in May, when the last five reached Egypt. 21 *Mira*, which had received a further five Gladiators in March-April 1941, was totally destroyed during the evacuation of Greece.

The Italians started the campaign with two *Gruppi* of CR.42s – Albanian-based 160° *Gruppo*, still partly equipped with CR.32s, and 150° *Gruppo*, which arrived from

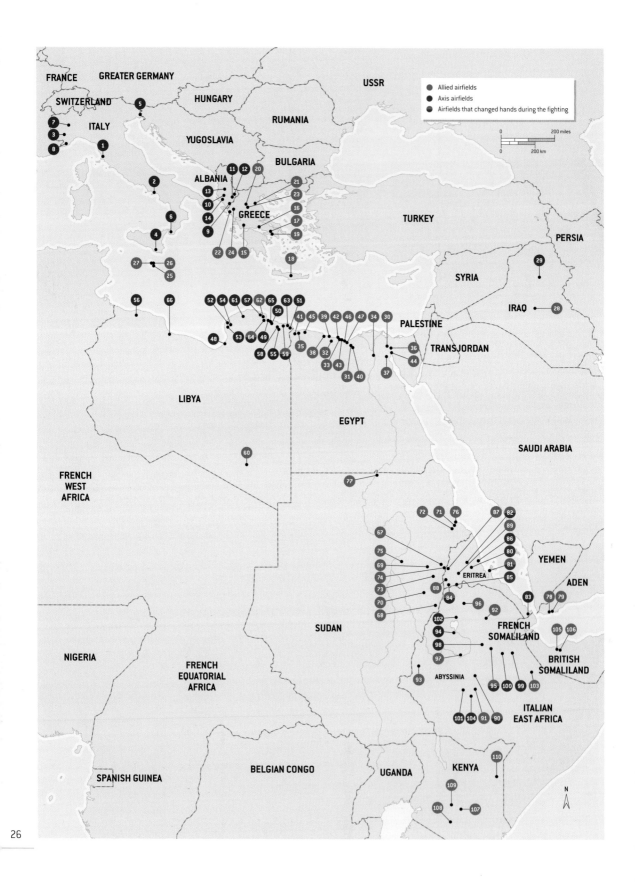

FRANCE

GREATER GERMANY

SWITZERLAND

ITALY

HUNGARY

USSR

RUMANIA

YUGOSLAVIA

BULGARIA

ALBANIA

GREECE

TURKEY

PERSIA

SYRIA

IRAQ

PALESTINE

TRANSJORDAN

LIBYA

EGYPT

SAUDI ARABIA

FRENCH WEST AFRICA

NIGERIA

FRENCH EQUATORIAL AFRICA

SPANISH GUINEA

SUDAN

ERITREA

YEMEN

ADEN

FRENCH SOMALILAND

BRITISH SOMALILAND

ABYSSINIA

ITALIAN EAST AFRICA

BELGIAN CONGO

UGANDA

KENYA

Allied airfields
Axis airfields
Airfields that changed hands during the fighting

0   200 miles
0   200 km

N

26

Italy

1. Campiglia (23° *Gruppo*, 9 July 1940) • 2. Capodichino (23° *Gruppo*, 9–10 July 1940) • 3. Cervere (23° *Gruppo*, 9–21 June 1940) • 4. Comiso (9° *Gruppo*, 1 July 1940; 23° *Gruppo*, 11 July–16 December 1940) • 5. Gorizia (9° *Gruppo*, 10 June 1940) • 6. Regio Calabria (23° *Gruppo*, 10–11 July 1940) • 7. Torino Mirafiori (9° *Gruppo*, June 1940, 23° *Gruppo*, 21–22 June and 25 June–9 July 1940) • 8. Villanova d'Albenga (23° *Gruppo*, 22–25 June 1940)

Albania

9. Gjirokastër Argyrokastron (150° *Gruppo*, November 1940) • 10. Berat (160° *Gruppo*, November 1940) • 11. Drenova (160° *Gruppo*, October 1940) • 12. Korçë (160° *Gruppo*, November 1940) • 13. Tirana (150° *Gruppo*, November 1940; 160° *Gruppo*, 21 November 1940) • 14. Vlorë (150° *Gruppo*, November 1940)

Greece and Crete

15. Agrinio (No. 112 Sqn RAF, 15–16 April 1941) • 16. Amphiklia/Lodi (21 *Mira*, 16–19 April 1941) • 17. Elefsina (Eleusis) (No. 80 Sqn RAF, 19–23 November 1940; Det. No. 80 Sqn RAF and No. 112 Sqn RAF, 23 January–18 February 1941; 21 *Mira*, 19–20 April 1941) • 18. Heraklion (No. 112 Sqn RAF, 22 April–31 May 1941) • 19. Kalamaki (No. 112 Sqn RAF, 16–22 April 1941) • 20. Kalambaka/Vassiliki (21 *Mira*) • 21. Làrisa (Larissa) (No. 80 Sqn RAF, 4 December 1940–16 January 1941) • 22. Paramythia (Det. No. 80 Sqn RAF; Det. No. 112 Sqn RAF; 21 *Mira*, April 1941) • 23. Trikala (Trikkala) (Det. No. 80 Sqn RAF; No. 80 Sqn RAF, 23 November–4 December 1940) • 24. Ioannina (Yanina) (Det. No. 80 Sqn RAF; Det. No. 112 Sqn RAF; 21 *Mira*, from 23 December 1940; No. 80 Sqn RAF, 16 January–27 February 1941; No. 112 Sqn RAF, 18 February–15 April 1941)

Malta

25. Far (Hal Far Station Flight, No. 261 Sqn RAF) • 26. Luqa (Hal Far Station Flight, No. 261 Sqn RAF) • 27. Ta'Quali (Takali) (Hal Far Station Flight, No. 261 Sqn RAF)

Iraq

28. Al Habbaniyah (Det. No. 94 Sqn RAF; 'A' Squadron, Habbaniyah Air Striking Force, May 1941) • 29. Kirkuk (*Squadriglia Speciale Iraq*)

Egypt

30. Abu Sueir (No. 80 Sqn RAF, 8–18 November 1940) • 31. Amiriya (No. 80 Sqn RAF, to 22 August 1940; No. 112 Sqn RAF, 1–23 January 1941); No. 94 Sqn RAF, 19–22 April 1941) • 32. Bir Kenayis (Det. No. 80 Sqn RAF) • 33. Gerawla (Det. No. 33 Sqn RAF; No. 112 Sqn RAF, 17 July–3 September 1940; No. 3 Sqn RAAF, from 2 November 1940) • 34. Helwan (No. 33 Sqn RAF, 25 June–22 September 1940; No. 112 Sqn RAF, to 17 July 1940; No. 3 Sqn RAAF) • 35. Ikingi Maryut (No. 3 Sqn RAAF, from 21 November 1940) • 36. Ismailia (No. 94 Sqn RAF, 22 April–29 August 1941) • 37. Kasfareet (No. 237 Sqn RAF, 24 August–21 September 1941) • 38. LG 'Y' (Det. No. 112 Sqn RAF, from 17 August 1940) • 39. LG 'Z'/Matruh West (Det. No. 112 Sqn RAF, from 17 August 1940 and from 14 September 1940) • 40. LG 30 (Det. No. 112 Sqn RAF, 3–7 September 1940) • 41. LG 79 (Det. No. 112 Sqn RAF, 14–31 December 1940) • 42. Mersa Matruh (No. 33 Sqn RAF, to 17 June 1940) • 43. Port Tewfik (No. 3 Sqn RAAF, from 23 August 1940) • 44. Qasaba (No. 33 Sqn RAF, 17–25 June 1940) • 45. Sidi Barrani (Det. No. 33 Sqn RAF; Det. No. 80 Sqn RAF, June 1940; Det. No. 112 Sqn RAF, from 3 August 1940; No. 80 Sqn RAF, 22–31 August 1940) •46. Sidi Haneish North (No. 112 Sqn RAF, 7 September–31 December 1940) • 47. Sidi Haneish South (No. 80 Sqn RAF, 31 August–8 November 1940)

Libya

48. Agedabia (151° *Gruppo*, to 21 January 1941) • 49. Ain el-Gazala T4 (9° *Gruppo*, 16–25 December 1940; 10° *Gruppo*, 16 December 1940–5 January 1941) • 50. Ain el-Gazala Z1 (23° *Gruppo*, 19 December 1940–5 January 1941) • 51. Amseat A3 (151° *Gruppo*, 30 October–11 December 1940) • 52. Benghazi-Berka K (10° *Gruppo*, 30 June–22 July 1940; 9° *Gruppo*, 13 July–8 August 1940; 8° *Gruppo*, 22 July–10 September and 15–20 December 1940; 13° *Gruppo*, 9 August–12 September 1940; 23° *Gruppo*, 7–9 January 1941) • 53. Benghazi K2 (23° *Gruppo*, 9 January–4 February 1941) • 54. Benghazi-Benina

(151° *Gruppo*, from 27 January 1941) • 55. Bir el-Gobi (10° *Gruppo*, from August 1940) • 56. Castelbenito (13° *Gruppo*, to 18 June 1940; 151° *Gruppo*, 8–15 September 1940; 23° *Gruppo*, 16–19 December 1940) • 57. Derna N1 (9° *Gruppo*, 12–16 December 1940; 10° *Gruppo*, 14–16 December 1940; 23° *Gruppo*, 6–7 January 1941) • 58. El Adem T3 (13° *Gruppo*, 1 July–9 August 1940; 10° *Gruppo*, from 22 July 1940 and from September 1940; 9° *Gruppo*, 8 August–12 December 1940; 8° *Gruppo*, 10–19 September 1940; 151° *Gruppo*, 15 September–30 October 1940) • 59. Gambut G (8° *Gruppo*, 10 September 1940; 13° *Gruppo*, from 12 September 1940; No. 3 Sqn RAAF, to 24 January 1941) • 60. Kufra (Det. No. 237 Sqn RAF) • 61. Maraua R (151° *Gruppo*, 21–27 January 1941) • 62. Martuba N3 (No. 3 Sqn RAAF, from 25 January 1941) • 63. Menastir M (8° *Gruppo*, 19 September–15 December 1940) • 64. Tmini M2 (23° *Gruppo*, 5–6 January 1941; No. 3 Sqn RAAF, 24–25 January 1941) • 65. Tobruk T2 (8° *Gruppo*, 4 June–22 July 1940; 10° *Gruppo*, to 30 June 1940; 13° *Gruppo*, 18 June–1 July 1940; 151° *Gruppo*, from 11 December 1940) • 66. Uadi Tamet (23° *Gruppo*, from 4 February 1941)

Sudan

67. ALG 'Aroma' (No. 1 Sqn SAAF, December 1940) • 68. ALG 'Heston' (No. 1 Sqn SAAF, November and December 1940; 'K' Flight, No. 112 Sqn RAF, November 1940) • 69. ALG 'Oxo' (No. 1 Sqn SAAF, January 1941) 8 70. ALG 'Pretoria' (No. 1 Sqn SAAF, December 1940) • 71. ALG 'Summit' (Det. No. 112 Sqn RAF; 'B' (later 'K') Flight, No. 112 Sqn RAF) • 72. Erkowit (Det. No. 112 Sqn RAF) • 73. Kashim el Girba (No. 1 Sqn SAAF, December 1940) • 74. Kassala (No. 1 Sqn SAAF, January 1941) • 75. Khartoum (No. 1 Sqn SAAF, August 1940) • 76. Port Sudan (Det. No. 112 Sqn RAF; 'B' (later 'K') Flight, No. 112 Sqn RAF; No. 1 Sqn SAAF, September 1940) • 77. Wadi Halfa (No. 237 Sqn RAF, 30 May–24 August 1941)

Aden

78. Little Aden (Det. No. 94 Sqn RAF) • 79. Sheikh Othman (No. 94 Sqn RAF, to 19 April 1941)

Eritrea (Italian East Africa)

80. Adi Ugri (413ª *Squadriglia*, September 1940) • 81. Agordat (412ª *Squadriglia*, January 1941; Det. No. 237 Sqn RAF; No. 1 Sqn SAAF, February 1941; 'K' Flight, No. 112 Sqn RAF, March 1941) • 82. Asmara (412ª *Squadriglia*; No. 237 Sqn RAF, 7 April–30 May 1941) • 83. Assab (413ª *Squadriglia*, 10 June 1940; 414ª *Squadriglia*, July 1940) • 84. Barentu (412ª *Squadriglia*; No. 237 Sqn RAF, 9–27 March 1941) • 85. Gura (412ª *Squadriglia*; 414ª *Squadriglia*, June 1940) • 86. Massawa (412ª *Squadriglia*) • 87. Sabderat (No. 1 Sqn SAAF, January 1941) • 88. Tessenei (No. 1 Sqn SAAF, January 1941) • 89. Umritsar (No. 237 Sqn RAF, 27 March–7 April 1941)

Ethiopia (Italian East Africa)

90. Addis Ababa (413ª *Squadriglia*, September 1940 and April 1941; No. 3 Sqn SAAF, April 1941) • 91. Algato (No. 3 Sqn SAAF, June 1941) • 92. Alomata (No. 3 Sqn SAAF, August 1941) • 93. Azzoza (No. 1 Sqn SAAF, September and November 1940; 'K' Flight, No. 112 Sqn RAF, November 1940) • 94. Bahr Dahr (412ª *Squadriglia*) • 95. Dessie-Combolocia (413ª *Squadriglia*, September 1940 and 5 April 1941; 412ª *Squadriglia*, 8 April 1941; No. 3 Sqn SAAF, July 1941) • 96. Dabat (No. 3 Sqn SAAF, October 1941) • 97. Debra Marcos (No. 3 Sqn SAAF, April 1941) • 98. Dessie (413ª *Squadriglia*, September 1940 and 5 April 1941) • 99. Dire Daua (413ª *Squadriglia*, July 1940; 110ª *Squadriglia*, January 1941) • 100. Gauani (413ª *Squadriglia*, 28 March 1941) • 101. Gimma (110ª *Squadriglia*, 24 March–5 June 1941; 413ª *Squadriglia*, April 1941) • 102. Gondar (413ª *Squadriglia*, August 1940 and October1941) • 103. Jijigga (No. 3 Sqn SAAF, April 1941) • 104. Sciasciamanna (413ª *Squadriglia*, 7 April 1941)

British Somaliland

105. Berbera (Det. No. 94 Sqn RAF) • 106. Laferug (Det. No. 94 Sqn RAF)

Kenya

107. Archer's Post (No. 2 Sqn SAAF, 1940) • 108. Nairobi (No. 2 Sqn SAAF, 1940) • 109. Nanyuki (No. 2 Sqn SAAF, 1940) • 110. Ndege's Nest (No. 2 Sqn SAAF, 1940)

Italy at the beginning of November. These units remained the only ones to operate over Greece, as G.50s and C.200s were now starting to reach the frontline in sufficient numbers. The monoplane fighters soon proved themselves to be less vulnerable than the Fiat biplanes, so the new reinforcement units for the sector were to fly them too, rather than *Falcos*. 150° *Gruppo* converted to C.200s during March, and only 160° *Gruppo* fought with the CR.42 until the end of the campaign, later moving to North Africa until year's end.

EAST AFRICA

In East Africa the first clashes between the CR.42 and the Gladiator came in July 1940 when 414ª *Squadriglia* defended the coastal airfield of Assab against raiders from No. 94 Sqn. In August, while the ten Gladiators of No. 112 Sqn's 'B' Flight became an independent unit christened 'K' Flight, the first nine brand-new Gladiators of No. 1 Sqn SAAF, which had just completed its training in Egypt, reached Kenya under Maj Noel Gray Niblock-Stuart. Nine more Gladiators from the same unit, under Maj Schalk van Schalkwyk, went to Khartoum. The South Africans were to acquire 12 additional second-hand Gladiator IIs and a solitary Mk I from RAF units before the campaign ended in 1941. Encounters between CR.42s and Gladiators over this vast sector were quite rare, the only exception being during the opening few days of the first Allied offensive of the war (against the border town of Metemma) in November 1940.

The unit in Kenya was re-formed as No. 2 Sqn SAAF at the end of September, but it had to give all of its Gladiators back to No. 1 Sqn SAAF in November. During December 'K' Flight sent most of its aeroplanes to Egypt, together with a detachment

Capitano Mario Visintini poses for the photographer in front of his personal aeroplane (a rare example of a radio-equipped CR.42) on Asmara airfield in January 1941. With him is 'Chica', the dog he adopted in Spain which became the mascot of 412ª *Squadriglia*. Visintini was the highest-scoring biplane fighter ace of World War II. (*Archivio Maria Giovanna Mengaziol*, via Enrico Neami)

from No. 94 Sqn to help in the pending offensive, leaving No. 1 Sqn SAAF as the only Gladiator-equipped unit over the frontline.

When the offensive against Italian East Africa started at the end of January 1941, No. 1 Sqn SAAF (now mainly equipped with newly arrived Hurricanes) still had some Gladiators on hand – at least seven on 30 January 1941. The biplanes saw a lot of action in a series of battles to gain air superiority over Eritrea, but by the middle of February they had been almost completely replaced by Hurricanes. 'K' Flight, now back in action, became the only unit flying the Gladiator over the frontline, together with No. 237 Sqn – a Rhodesian air cooperation unit that had received some fighters passed on by the South Africans.

The remaining Italian forces were now besieged in the area of Gondar in northwestern Ethiopia, and the task of controlling them fell to No. 3 Sqn SAAF, with whom Gladiators remained in service in 'A' Flight until November 1941 – the very last Gladiators to see active service in a Commonwealth fighter squadron.

Throughout this period the Italians, who had started the campaign with a complement of 26 CR.42s (six more were unserviceable), struggled to maintain the line's strength. They resorted to sending disassembled replacement aeroplanes to East Africa inside specially modified Savoia-Marchetti SM.82s of 149° *Gruppo Trasporti* (Transport) which, starting from Rome Urbe Airport, reached Asmara through Benghazi. The Italian official history states that by the end of March 1941 the *Gruppo* had transported 51 new CR.42s to East Africa, with a record 15 making the journey that month alone. Conversely, an analysis of flights made by the unit during 1940 shows that only 11 aeroplanes were transported in the four-month period between 23 August and 31 December. The remainder arrived in 1941, so the grand total in-theatre was probably overestimated.

Demolished on the ground or shot down by Hurricanes patrolling over their bases, the Italian fighter *Squadriglie* disappeared in April 1941. Only three CR.42s remained in Gondar, fighting from there until it fell to the Allies.

UNIT ORGANISATION

The basic Italian fighter unit was the *squadriglia*. With a strength of 12 aeroplanes and around 16 pilots, the 'theoretical' *squadriglia*, commanded by a capitano, was composed of two-thirds non-commissioned officers (marescialli, sergenti maggiori and sergenti) and one-third officers (sottotenenti and tenenti). In fact the strength of a typical Italian fighter *squadriglia* at the beginning of the war was around nine or ten fighters – a number that, during operations, tended to reduce quickly to a half, as reserves were generally not immediately available. A *squadriglia* could be further divided into sections of three or four, generally commanded by a tenente.

Three *squadriglie* formed a *gruppo*, commanded by a maggiore. The strength of a *gruppo* thus comprised between 36 (theoretical) and 27 (actual) aeroplanes. It was very common for the *gruppi* to move and fight as independent units. This was also due to the fact that the *gruppo* was the smallest-sized unit still able to guarantee a combat force of around 15 aeroplanes fit for daily operations (Italian fighter units rarely had

A CR.42 of 75ª *Squadriglia, 23°
Gruppo* makes a low sweep over
Comiso airfield in the autumn of
1940. Owing to the muddy
conditions then afflicting the
base, all of the CR.42s in this
photograph have had their wheel
spats removed, as they were
prone to clogging. (Maria Teresa
Bobba)

more than 50 per cent of the nominal strength serviceable on a daily basis). Fifteen
was the number of aircraft deemed necessary to successfully perform free sweeps and
escort missions.

Two *gruppi* formed a *stormo*, the latter being commanded by a tenente colonnello
or a colonnello. A variable number of *stormi* and independent *gruppi* could be joined
to form a *brigata aerea* or a *divisione aerea*, commanded, respectively, by a *generale di
brigata aerea* and a *generale di divisione aerea*. These units were the biggest to host the
same aircraft type. At a superior level there were the *zone aeree* and the *aeronautiche*,
which collected together all the units based in a certain area. At the beginning of the
war there were *Aeronautica della Sardegna, Aeronautica dell'Albania, Aeronautica della*

Pilots of 368ª *Squadriglia* pose in
front of newly arrived CR.42s.
Standing sixth from right is
Capitano Bruno Locatelli,
Sottotenente Furio Lauri is third
from right, Sergente Maggiore
Davide Colauzzi is fourth from
right, Sergente Mario Turchi is
sixth from left and Tenente Carlo
Bongiovanni is seated atop the
cowling. (Enrico Locatelli)

Libia, *Aeronautica dell'Egeo*, *Aeronautica dell'Africa Orientale Italiana* in East Africa and 4ª *Zona Aerea* covering Southeastern Italy. A larger group of *stormi* and *gruppi* of different kinds formed the biggest unit within the *Regia Aeronautica*, the *squadra aerea*.

The RAF's basic fighting unit was the squadron. Formations above this level were much less formal and less structured than in other air forces. The size of the squadron was generally set so that it was able to operate at least 12 aircraft on a regular basis. In the Middle East, the initial equipment of a fighter squadron was established at 16 aircraft, with an immediate reserve of eight machines, usually but not always held by each unit. Additional reserves were kept at air depots and maintenance units.

Squadrons were subdivided into flights, but these usually operated only as a part of the squadron. However, in the Middle East it was not uncommon for flights to operate individually, 'B' Flight of No. 112 Sqn in Sudan being an example. A squadron was usually commanded by a squadron leader, while flights were commanded by flight lieutenants. Other operational ranks for pilots were sergeant, flight sergeant, warrant officer, pilot officer and flying officer. Squadrons could be grouped into wings for operational purposes, and wings were brought together administratively into groups. Squadrons were interchangeable between wings.

RAAF and SAAF squadrons were similar to the RAF ones, even if the ranks in the SAAF units differed from those of the RAF and RAAF, being more similar to those in the British Army – second lieutenant, lieutenant, captain. Squadrons were usually commanded by a major.

Gladiator I K7974/RT-O of No. 112 Sqn in 1940. Plt Off Oliver Green claimed a Ca.133 destroyed over Gedaref, Sudan, on 1 August 1940 while flying this aircraft. It was later transferred to 'K' Flight and was destroyed in an accident on 22 December 1940. (Andrew Thomas)

THE COMBATANTS

ITALIAN PILOT TRAINING

Fighter pilots of the *Regia Aeronautica* could be permanent officers (Ufficiali in Servizio Permanente Effettivo or S.P.E.), short-commission officers (ufficiali di complemento) or non-commissioned officers (sottoufficiali). The Ufficiali in S.P.E. were trained at the Air Force Academy in Caserta, and it was from here that a small number of individuals were chosen to fill the flying ranks within the air force. It was also possible for a short-commission officer to enter the permanent officer corps as a result of war merit. Ufficiali di complemento and sottoufficiali constituted the bulk of the air force. The three groups underwent training programmes of different length and quality, the greatest differences being the levels of theoretical study that was undertaken, while flying school was quite similar for all pilots.

Roughly speaking, flying school was divided into two main levels called *Periodi*. At the end of the 1° *Periodo* the pupils gained their wings and became pilots. At the end of the 2° *Periodo*, also called the *Scuola di Specialità* (Specialised Flying School), they became military pilots, being awarded their crowned eagle badge and promoted to sottotenenti piloti at the officers' schools and sergenti piloti in the NCO pilots' schools. They were then sent to the operational units that were tasked with completing their training on the aircraft the pilots were destined to fly in the frontline.

This two-level scheme always remained valid, even though the training programme evolved continuously from 1927, when, under Italo Balbo, the first *Scuola di Specialità* was created, until war's end, with a tendency for flying hours to increase steadily.

Originally, the 1° *Periodo* was left mainly to civilian flying schools, but from the mid-1930s onwards it was increasingly confined to specially created military schools. The 2° *Periodo* was always carried out in military schools dedicated to each field of operation – fighters, bombers and seaplanes.

Fighter training programmes were never particularly rich in flying hours. In 1939, for example, cockpit time in the 1° *Periodo* lasted some 60 hours, and only 20 hours for the 2° *Periodo*. These figures are representative of the highest totals attained in the 1930s, and are typical for the scholastic training of a CR.42 pilot during the period covered by this book. Short-commission officers and NCOs completed this training in about 14 months and then transferred to an operational unit for a period of 18 months, after which they could leave the air force to enter the reserve force. It took three years to train permanent officers, however, their flying school being situated at Capua airport, north of Naples.

Training principles also evolved during the interwar period. In 1925 the HQ of the *Regia Aeronautica* – then led by World War I ace Pier Ruggero Piccio – published the *Norme Provvisorie per l'addestramento e l'impiego dell'aviazione da caccia* (*Provisional rules for the training and employment of the fighter force*). This document stressed from the outset that, after learning how to fly an aeroplane, it was necessary for pilots to learn how to fire its guns. The individual training ended with navigation school. The text described the importance of a proper and continuous training in shooting, with camera guns being used against small parachutes, small balloons or drogues. Real guns were used against static targets on the ground and, finally, against moving targets in flight, such as small parachutes, small balloons and drogues.

Finally, the pilots were required to put into practice what they had learnt in the *finta caccia* (mock combat), using camera guns. The training hints contained in the *Norme* show that the concept of *serrare sotto* (open fire only at the minimum distance) was already well known, and reputed to be a sure factor for success, although it was not always applicable. This is not surprising when one remembers that World War I had only ended seven years prior to the publication of this document, and all the

CR.42 96-1 of 96ª *Squadriglia*, 9° *Gruppo* at Gorizia immediately before the war. (Secchiaroli via Fulvio Chianese)

CR.42 *FALCO* COCKPIT

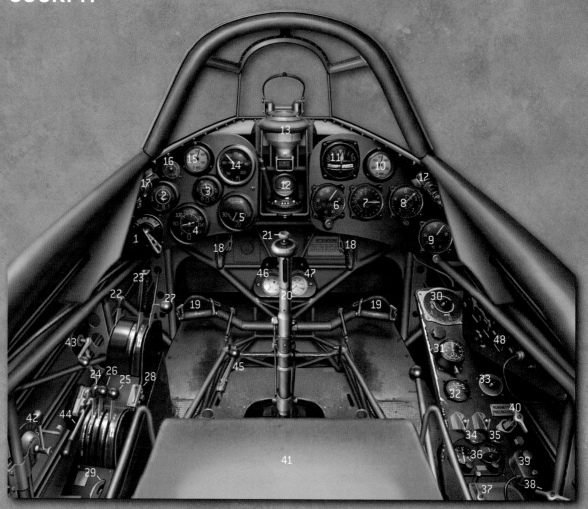

1. Ignition switch
2. Fuel pressure gauge
3. Oil pressure gauge
4. Oil temperature gauge
5. Tachometer
6. Air speed indicator
7. Rate-of-climb indicator
8. Altimeter
9. Air speed indicator (back up)
10. Right gun ammunition counter
11. Turn and bank indicator
12. Compass
13. San Giorgio Type B reflector gunsight
14. Manifold pressure indicator
15. Left gun ammunition counter
16. Engine fire warning indicator
17. Cockpit lights (x 2)
18. Gun charging handles

19. Rudder pedals
20. Control column
21. Gun firing button
22. Mixture control
23. Throttle
24. Propeller pitch control
25. Propeller RPM control
26. Oil cooler flap control
27. Carburettor mixture control
28. Propeller lever stop
29. Elevator trim wheel
30. Fuel lever indicator
31. Clock
32. Cylinder head temperature
33. Cylinder head temperature probe selector
34 & 35. Gun synchronisation gear coupling levers
36. Oxygen control panel

37. Engine starter power crank
38. Two-way selector for engine starting
39. Gunsight rheostat
40. Gun cocking mechanism
41. Pilot's seat
42. Auxiliary fuel tank cock
43. Main fuel tank cock
44. Manual fuel charging pump
45. CO_2 fire extinguisher lever
46. Brake pressure gauge
47. Pressurised air tank contents gauge
48. Light switch panel

lessons bloodily learned in that conflict were probably still alive in the memories of many pilots of the time.

The document repeatedly stressed the importance of fighting in formation, and described how to train the pilots in collective flight and combat because 'the era of individual combat had already finished during the previous war'. Many pages were devoted to this topic, listing hints learned during the previous war and pointing out again and again the importance of not losing contact during a combat.

Finally, in a note on in-flight communications, the document stated, 'in this most important field the pilots are still obliged to use flag signals, smoke signals and other conventional systems signals that are all not fully satisfactory, but things are going to change with the advent of more reliable and technically advanced RT [receiver/ transmitter] systems'.

This 1925 document shows that individualism in flight was discouraged as a result of previous war experience, the importance of tactical training to be able to make full use of numbers was clear, the importance of gunnery training and combat training was very clear and a training doctrine was fully developed. In 1936 a new version of the fighter pilot training manual was made available, entitled *Addestramento dell'Aviazione da Caccia* (*Fighter Training*). Smaller than the original one produced under Piccio, it was less detailed, expressing only general concepts.

Compared with the 1925 version, navigational training took priority over gunnery training, being the second step to be tackled after learning to fly, but the importance of gunnery training was not forgotten, with the additional note that 'shooting against drogues has to be developed to the maximum extent, being the exercise that gives a closer approximation to real shooting against live targets, while shooting against captive balloons has to be limited or considered only as a starting phase'. It is also interesting to note that, in an excess of wishful thinking, in-flight communication was considered only as RT communication, with no mention at all of other methods.

Most of the document was devoted to formation flying and aerobatics, but a final appendix stated that combat manoeuvres were to be considered the exception, while the rule was to be the surprise attack – great importance was given to the rate of fire and the accuracy of shooting. The manual showed which manoeuvres were useful in combat, with most aerobatics being explicitly described as 'not useful'. This 1936 document shows that the importance of RT communications was well understood, gunnery training theory had further developed in ten years and was at least in line with RAF practice and, while great emphasis was placed on aerobatics to create good pilots, it was already known that very few aerobatic manoeuvres could be profitably used in combat.

The Spanish Civil War, which started that year, brought another step forward in tactical learning that apparently was not yet formalised in a revised version of the Fighter Manual when the war started, but was summarised in an article written for the *Regia Aeronautica's* official magazine, *Rivista Aeronautica*, in May 1940. Apart from a detailed analysis of every type of formation used during the conflict by the units of the *Aviazione Legionaria*, it showed that the basic formation of the fighter force had to be changed from the three-aircraft *pattuglia* (vic) to the two-aircraft *coppia*, while the tactical unit to enter battle had to be increased from the nine-aircraft *squadriglia* to the 27-strong *gruppo*.

The *Regia Aeronautica's* participation in the Spanish Civil War resulted in the modernisation of its tactics and widespread operational experience among pilots, raising the capabilities of most veterans of that conflict to that of the best pilots of the great powers such as Britain, France and Germany, which had benefited from much better peacetime training. However, the war had also been a 'furnace' where billions of lire were 'burned' funding the fighting. For three years Italy had to maintain an operational force of around 600 aeroplanes in Spain and Ethiopia, while struggling at home to reinforce and modernise itself to be able to meet the needs of the pending war. This ultimately resulted in a restriction of flying hours and the lack of more realistic (and expensive) training for the majority of the pilots who remained in Italy.

The expenditure of the country's economic resources also adversely affected technical development in many ways. Indeed, it was probably one of the most significant contributory causes of the delay in the introduction into service of new monoplane fighters, and of the development of a reliable RT system with which to equip them.

In the end, despite the relatively updated theoretical concepts of tactical training, cost constraints relegated most pilots to an actual practice of close-formation aerobatics with very little shooting, mostly against static targets such as captive balloons. Apart from being quite ineffective, this training was also unnecessarily dangerous, and it caused the loss of many pilots in peacetime drills. In fact three of the top ten Italian aces of the Spanish Civil War, 'ace of aces' Sottotenente Bruno di Montegnacco and Capitani Enrico degli Incerti and Giuseppe Majone, lost their lives while performing aerobatics after the war. Majone was killed in a mid-air collision with Capitano Alfiero Mezzetti (another prominent *Aviazione Legionaria* pilot), who also lost his life.

If we add to this list the nine-victory ace and tactician Tenente Colonello Andrea Zotti, who also died in an aeroplane crash (though not linked to aerobatics), we have an idea of the drastic losses suffered by the *Regia Aeronautica* to non-operational causes even before the start of World War II. Additionally, the lack of a working RT system meant that no doctrine for its use in combat had yet been developed when the conflict broke out.

Although an elite group within the *Regia Aeronautica*, the fighter force could only cope with a short-length conflict. And although its pilots, in particular the veterans of the Spanish Civil War, were among the best in the world, its combat doctrine – studied and refined to apply to biplane units without RT communications – was far

Operating from rock-strewn Agedabia, in Libya, CR.42s of 366ª *Squadriglia*, 151° *Gruppo* taxi out for takeoff in 1940. (Renato Zavattini)

from the best. Pilots had to rely on outdated combat manuals and obsolescent equipment, which in turn directly affected the quality of the training given to the majority of those flying CR.42s.

RAF AND COMMONWEALTH PILOT TRAINING

In June 1940 the RAF was undergoing a vigorous process of rearmament and expansion that had started in 1936 and eventually saw the birth of a dedicated organisation to take care of the creation of new pilots – Training Command. The training scheme for RAF pilots also changed during the period leading up to the war, but in principle it was not so different from that of the *Regia Aeronautica*, being divided into two main periods of flying school instruction interspersed by a spell of theoretical military training.

For many of the pilots who would later see combat flying the Gladiator in Africa and Greece, the first period of instruction took place at an Elementary and Reserve Flying Training School (ERFTS), where they learned to fly in basic trainers such as the de Havilland Tiger Moth or similar types. Once they had earned their wings they endured a short period of theoretical military training in a Flying Training School (FTS). Here, the second level of training started, further divided in two sub-periods, Initial Training (IT) and Advanced Training (AT), both of which lasted three months. Pupils received instruction in a wide range of subjects that included theory of flight, rigging, engines, elementary wireless, meteorology, navigation and armament.

At the end of the IT they became military pilots, while the AT was done in operational aircraft types and ended with the Armament Practice Camp, where gunnery practice was finally carried out. The camps, very often located close to the sea, varied in length, sometimes lasting as long as two weeks. Here, the pupils could finally practise in actual firing against square cloth targets lying on the sand, or at towed drogues.

The total training period also varied, but it generally lasted about nine months. Flying hours changed during the period, but to make a comparison with the *Regia Aeronautica* it is known that in 1939 the typical RAF cadet underwent about 150 hours of training (50 hours of AT), before going to an operational unit, and it is possible that this total was even greater before the war started. The two top RAF Gladiator aces of the conflict, Flt Lt Thomas Pattle and Sgt William Vale, both went through this training programme, Vale having his second-level training in Egypt at No. 4 FTS at Abu Sueir – then the only such school outside Britain. They qualified as pilots in May and July 1937, respectively. Another outstanding RAF pilot of this period, Plt Off Vernon Woodward, joined the RAF in August 1938 and completed his training in March 1939. Despite a shorter training period, he followed exactly the same scheme of ERFTS and FTS.

RAF fighter doctrine also evolved in the interwar years. In 1933 the *Flying Training Manual* distributed to the pilots stressed above all the importance of morale, as well

GLADIATOR I/II COCKPIT

1. GM2 reflector gunsight
2. Cockpit light dimmer switch
3. R/T remote controller
4. Cockpit lights (x 2)
5. Oxygen controls and gauges
6. Throttle controls
7. Throttle lever friction adjuster
8. Carburettor cutout
9. Pitot tube heater switch
10. Emergency fuel cock lever
11. Oil cooler control
12. Turn and bank indicator
13. Engine starter button
14. Air speed indicator
15. Artificial horizon
16. Rate-of-climb

17. Altimeter
18. Direction indicator
19. Brake pressure gauge
20. RPM indicator
21. Oil pressure gauge
22. Boost gauge
23. Fuel gauge
24. Fuel pressure gauge
25. Cockpit door lock lever
26. Ignition switches
27. Fuel cock
28. Oil pressure gauge
29. Cylinder priming pump
30. Compass
31. Rudder pedals
32. Magneto switch

33. Elevator trim control wheel
34. Seat adjustment lever
35. Pilot's seat
36. Control column and spade grip
37. Gun firing button
38. Brake lever
39. 0.303-in. machine guns (x 2)
40. Engine cylinder head temperature gauge
41. Ammunition feed chutes (x 2)
42. Link ejection chutes (x 2)
43. Flaps control lever
44. Signalling switch box
45. Rudder pedals adjustment wheel

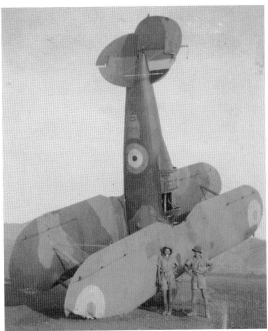

as the moral that it was necessary to maintain continuous offensive action against the enemy. Even flying skills and marksmanship were considered of lesser importance. Training had to instil in pupils the maximum possible self-confidence and conviction of their superiority as fighting pilots. After this (perhaps too ideological) premise, the real training programme started, divided into ground and flying activities.

Ground practice was centred primarily on guns and aiming, while flying practice had to start with basic aerobatics, always put into context with their effective use in combat, progressing immediately thereafter to firing practice and then to aerial tactics and aircraft recognition. The flying training was aimed at perfecting the piloting skills of the pupils, then developing all the skills necessary to aim the aircraft's weapons accurately and steadily while flying or diving, and to aim correctly at moving targets. Advanced training also had to provide some of the basics of one-versus-one aerial combat and formation combat. Nightfighter training was also provided.

In 1938 these instructions were replaced by an updated version, much influenced by the entry into service of the new high-speed eight-gun monoplanes that led RAF headquarters to believe that 'Manoeuvre at high speed in air fighting is not now practicable'. The primary task for fighters was now reputed to be the attacking of massed formations of unescorted bombers, and for this reason fighting area attacks were developed and most of the tactical training was carried out practising them. The majority of the Gladiator pilots who met CR.42s in combat at the end of 1940 had been trained using the 1933 manual as a guide.

The RAF programme was clearly superior to that taught to *Regia Aeronautica* students, in particular if they had been trained in accordance with the 1936 Italian manual. If in the end (taking into account the great importance of proper training) this did not result in the RAF having clear advantage over their Italian counterparts in combat, this was primarily because British pilots did very little real gunnery training

Flg Off Richard Acworth of No. 112 Sqn claimed two and one shared destroyed CR.42s while flying the Gladiator in North Africa in the autumn of 1940. He claimed two additional Fiat G.50bis in a Gladiator over Greece in the spring of 1941. In total, Acworth claimed seven and one shared destroyed. (*Ian Acworth*)

Gladiator N5830 of No. 1 Sqn SAAF probably on 30 January 1941, when it was damaged in a forced landing at Sabderat, in Eritrea. (SAAF Museum)

(only a few hours during the Armament Practice Camps) due to cost constraints. Most of the good principles expressed in the manual remained little more than theory for RAF pilots, while their Italian contemporaries gained invaluable practical experience of real combat in Spain. This in turn helped raise the standard of many Italian fighter pilots to that of their better-trained RAF foes.

The RAF was not the only Commonwealth air force to fly the Gladiator in combat. As recounted earlier, No. 3 Sqn RAAF and No. 1 Sqn SAAF also soldiered on with the biplane fighters that they had received from the RAF's Egyptian aircraft depots in the summer of 1940.

Despite the presence of many South African aces in the ranks of the Royal Flying Corps during World War I, the SAAF fighter force had totally disappeared in the interwar years. Indeed, it was not until 1936 that fighters were once again seen over the skies of the Union in the form of seven Hawker Fury IIs. In the meantime only a handful of South Africans had been able to participate in the SAAF's pilot training course, most of them, like Thomas Pattle, having to move to Britain to fulfil their desire to fly.

Despite this shortcoming the small but élite nucleus of a well-trained permanent force was formed, and No. 1 Sqn SAAF was finally established in August 1938. Within this force, consisting only of officers, were some of the best fighter pilots to see service in the early years of the war. However, they were almost devoid of any realistic fighter training. It is known that they adopted the British doctrine of 1939, centred on fighting area attacks, but as far as fighter tactics were concerned pilots had to find out for themselves, starting from May 1940 in Egypt, when they began the transition to Gladiators. They also carried out more realistic gunnery training from then on too.

The RAAF was in a better position, having been able to raise a force of nine Permanent Air Force squadrons in the interwar years up to 1939. The pilots in these units had been carefully selected, and those in No. 3 Sqn were no exception. The problem here, however, was that the unit had originally been formed for air cooperation with the Australian Army, and it had been transferred to Egypt in August to convert to Westland Lysanders. It was not until 16 September 1940 that HQ Middle East signalled that two flights from the squadron were to convert to Gladiators. The pilots began to receive them a few days later, and despite doing plenty of air-to-air gunnery and other tactical training, they were still 'green' on the type when they commenced operations from Gerawla in the middle of November 1940.

The last unit to see combat on the Gladiator was 21 *Mira* of the Royal Hellenic Air Force. Very little is known about this small band of pilots and their commander, Sminagos Ioannis Kellas, during the period in which they operated the Gladiator. However, the sheer fact that they continued to hold the line in a handful of worn out biplanes until the last day of the campaign says a lot about their skills, and their valour.

MARIO VISINTINI

Born in Parenzo d'Istria (now Porec, in Croatia) on 26 April 1913 into a family of Italian heritage, Mario Visintini was to become the first ace of the *Regia Aeronautica*, and the top biplane ace of World War 2. He was also a legend to all Italians living in East Africa during the conflict, and to the refugees from Istria after the war. Despite this, the documents now available to enable researchers to describe much of his combat career do not confirm that he claimed a single victory against a Gloster Gladiator. This is mainly due to the nature of the missions flown by Visintini in East Africa, which were mostly interceptions of unescorted bombers. However, it could also be due to the fact that not all of Visintini's 16 or probably 17 claims have yet been identified, and it is likely that some of those for which details are lacking were gained against Gladiators.

The son of an agricultural expert, Mario Visintini tried to enter the *Regia Accademia Aeronautica* but failed the medical test because he was declared to be 'too weak and susceptible'. Returning home, he enrolled in the University of Bologna to study Agricultural Sciences, but on 24 September 1935 he left the school to join the air force as a short-commission officer, gaining his civilian pilot's licence on 30 May 1936 and finally joining 4º *Stormo* at the end of the year. In November 1937 he went to Spain as a volunteer, and in ten months of operations in the ranks of XVI *Gruppo Cucaracha* Visintini distinguished himself as an outstanding pilot, also claiming a number of individual victories. At least two of them are documented – an I-16 on 24 August 1938 and an I-15 of 1ª *Escuadrilla Chatos* on 5 September that same year.

Promoted In Servizio Permanente Effettivo in September 1939 for his efforts in Spain, Visintini was sent to East

Africa to join the ranks of 412ª *Squadriglia* in April 1940. Flying from Gura on 12 June 1940, he shot down Vickers Wellesley K7747 of No 223 Sqn. After returning to Massawa, he was leading a four-aircraft section tasked to defend the base when he shot down four more Wellesleys on 30 June (L2654 of No. 223 Sqn), 3 July (L2652 of No. 14 Sqn), possibly 26 August (K7731 of No. 223 Sqn) and 1 September (L2669 of No. 14 Sqn), the last victory qualifying him as an ace.

Returning to Gura on 20 September, he claimed four Blenheims of No. 45 Sqn during five combats fought in a few days (three of them, L6665, L8463 and L8502, are confirmed in British sources). Visintini claimed two more Blenheims, R3593 and R2770 of No. 14 Sqn, on 26 November and 4 December, and Wellesley L2690 of No. 223 Sqn during a night interception on 15 December. On 7 February 1941 he was officially credited with his 15th and 16th victories (probably Wellesleys K8525 and K7759 of No. 47 Sqn). His 17th, and final, 'victory' was the Hurricane of ace Flt Lt Ken Driver, which he almost shot down on 10 February. Thus up to now it has been possible to identify 15 of Visintini's 17 victories. The two missing ones could be Gladiators, probably over Gallabat in the afternoon of 6 November 1940.

At this stage Visintini was promoted to capitano on the strength of his record in combat and recommended for the gold medal for bravery 'a vivente' (not posthumously). This was a rare recognition during wartime. The recommendation for the award, written on 9 February, when the ace's score stood at 16, described his numerous aerial and ground victories.

On the afternoon of 11 February 1941 Visintini took off together with his loyal wingmen, Sergente Maggiore Luigi Baron and Tenente Ubaldo Buzzi, to patrol over the Keren area and strafe enemy troops. After an indecisive combat against two Hurricanes, Buzzi, who had just arrived in the sector, became disoriented and Baron remained with him, both pilots landing in the Saberguma plain, south of Massawa. Visintini, who had by now returned to Asmara, took off immediately to guide his pilots back to base, despite poor visibility in the mountains around the airfield. He duly crashed on the slopes of Mount Bizen near the town of Nefasit, being killed instantly. An award of the gold medal for bravery followed his demise.

Visintini remained the *Regia Aeronautica's* top scorer for many months after his death. His victories, most of which can be confirmed in Commonwealth records, were obtained flying a biplane on a front where opportunities to score where not so plentiful. The Italian Air force subsequently bestowed his name on Rivolto airfield, home of the famous *Frecce Tricolori* aerobatic team.

JOSEPH FRASER

Born in Colombo, Ceylon, in 1915, Joe Fraser was sent to the UK for his education, attending Malvern College and Pembroke College, Cambridge, where he served in the University Air Squadron. As a consequence he was commissioned in the Reserve of Air Force Officers as a pilot officer on 15 December 1936, transferring to the RAF Volunteer Reserve (RAFVR) on 1 January 1938, and then to the RAF. Fraser received a permanent commission as a pilot officer on 6 September 1938. On 16 May 1939 he was posted to No. 112 Sqn when this unit was formed aboard the aircraft carrier HMS *Argus* in Portsmouth. Immediately after its formation the unit was sent to Egypt.

When the war started in North Africa on 10 June 1940, No. 112 Sqn, based at Helwan, 15 miles south of Cairo, was solely responsible for the defence of Egypt's capital. During the initial combats against the Italians in North Africa, Flg Off Fraser claimed two SM.79s unconfirmed destroyed and one damaged. Promoted to flight commander prior to No. 112 Sqn's move to Greece in early 1941, he was heavily involved in action over the Albanian Front during late February/early March, claiming nine victories. Fraser was awarded a DFC before month-end following these successes.

During the large-scale combats on 28 February 1941 between Tepelenë and the coast, the RAF made claims for five BR.20s, three SM.79s, 13 CR.42s (plus three probables) and six G.50bis destroyed and three probables. In fact, only four BR.20s of 37° *Stormo* B.T. had been lost and several damaged, one SM.79 of the 104° *Gruppo* damaged and one CR.42 of 160° *Gruppo* and one G.50bis of 24° *Gruppo* lost. The *Regia Aeronautica* claimed six Gladiators, plus two probables, and one 'Spitfire', whereas only a single Gladiator of No. 112 Sqn had been downed. Of these claims, one CR.42 and one G.50bis were credited to Fraser as his first confirmed victories.

On 4 March Italian warships sailed down the Albanian coast under the cover of a strong fighter escort. A strike was ordered in the afternoon by RAF Blenheims, escorted by fighters. In the ensuing combat the RAF claimed seven G.50bis and four probables and three CR.42s and one probable, while losing two Hurricanes. 24° *Gruppo* lost two CR.42s and had a third one damaged, while claiming four Gladiators, one Spitfire and one Fairey Battle. Fraser claimed a G.50bis destroyed and another shared destroyed.

On 9 March a new Italian offensive began in Greece, No. 112 Sqn clashing with Italian fighters and bombers. Fraser claimed one G.50bis and one BR.20 (making him an ace), and in total the squadron was credited with eight G.50s destroyed and one probable and one BR.20 destroyed and one probable, while losing a Gladiator. In fact, the 'G.50s' were C.200s of 22° *Gruppo*, which lost only one aircraft. Two or three BR.20s were damaged, against a claim of four Gladiators by the bombers' gunners.

On 11 March No. 112 Sqn escorted Blenheims on a raid in the Bousi area. They clashed with G.50bis and claimed seven shot down and one probable without loss. Fraser claimed one G.50bis destroyed and another damaged. 24° *Gruppo* lost four aircraft and claimed one Blenheim and one Gladiator shot down.

Two days later Fraser claimed three CR.42s destroyed during an offensive patrol. His squadron claimed ten CR.42s and two probables and a 'G.50bis' without loss. The Italians claimed four Gladiators and a Hurricane shot down, for the loss of two CR.42s but no C.200s. Fraser attacked a CR.42 whose pilot had not seen him, reporting that it burst into flames and crashed near Bousi. He then attacked another CR.42, which flick-rolled and dived away. Following it down, he got in two long bursts, after which the aircraft levelled off and lost speed, its pilot slumped forward in the cockpit. The fighter dived vertically into the ground north of Corovode. Fraser climbed up to 8,000ft and attacked another CR.42, firing at it until it burst into flames and was destroyed. Although his own aircraft was badly shot up, Fraser returned to base. In his combat report he remarked that the CR.42 pilots tried to flick-roll when attacked. The next day Fraser claimed his last victory in Greece when he downed a G.50.

On 13 June 1941 Fraser left No. 112 Sqn and was posted to No 71 Operational Training Unit as an instructor, being promoted to squadron leader. He became a wing commander on 1 July 1944. Towards the end of the war Fraser flew Spitfires from Northolt airfield until the end of August 1945, when he was posted to Ankara, Turkey, to train Turkish Air Force pilots to fly jet aircraft. On 11 August 1946 he was killed in an automobile accident in Ankara.

COMBAT

NORTH AFRICA

The shooting war started on the morning of 11 June 1940 with the first raids by British bombers on the Italian airfields. The first clash between the CR.42 and the Gladiator came a few days later, on 14 June, over the Libyan/Egyptian border, when three of 10° *Gruppo*'s fighters intercepted a Gladiator of No. 33 Sqn and claimed to have shot it down. In fact no losses were recorded on this occasion by the RAF unit.

Five days later No. 33 Sqn pilots claimed two CR.42s destroyed for the loss of N5888, flown by Sgt R. L. Green, who was killed in action when a patrol of four Gladiator IIs, strengthened by a single Hurricane, surprised a flight of six CR.42s of the same 10° *Gruppo*. In this combat the Italians lost two *Falcos*. One of them, MM4401, was forced-landed by the *Gruppo*'s CO, Tenente Colonello Armando Piragino, who was taken prisoner of war (PoW). The pilot of the other CR.42, who lost his life, was Sergente Maggiore Ugo Corsi, one of the *Regia Aeronautica*'s best aerobatic flyers. It should be noted that on this occasion at least one and perhaps both of the Fiats were shot down by the Hurricane, flown by future 14-victory ace Peter Wykeham-Barnes.

The border skirmishes continued without further encounters between the two biplane types until the beginning of July, when No. 33 Sqn, reinforced by a section from No. 112 Sqn, began to patrol more aggressively over the *Regia Aeronautica*'s advanced airstrips. During the morning of 4 July 1940 three Gladiators met two CR.42s of the 8° *Gruppo* and claimed them both destroyed. Italian sources confirm

Sergente Ernesto Pavan in CR.42 92-8 of 92ª *Squadriglia*, 8° *Gruppo* in the summer of 1940. (Roberto Pavan)

that Tenente Giovanni Tadini and Sergente Maggiore Arturo Cardano were shot down, both being taken prisoner. Several hours later a patrol of six Gladiators flew directly over the Italian advanced airstrip at Menastir, from where a detachment of 8° *Gruppo* was operating. Five pilots of the latter unit scrambled to intercept the British fighter and were duly slaughtered when the RAF pilots dived on them. Capitano Franco Lavelli and Sergenti Maggiori Agostino Fausti and Trento Cecchi were all killed, while Sottotenente Nunzio De Fraia bailed out wounded. Only Tenente Domenico Bevilaqua was able to escape, wounded, in his damaged aeroplane.

During this action the RAF lost N5751, piloted by Flg Off W. B. Price-Owen. The fighter had been shot up during the engagement, forcing the pilot to bail out during the return flight. Nine victories were claimed by No. 33 Sqn, including four by Flg Off A. G. Worcester (a pilot attached to the unit from No. 112 Sqn) and a double by Flt Sgt L. Cottingham, who had also scored a victory that morning.

Despite a certain degree of perhaps unavoidable overclaiming, the combat was indeed a great victory for the RAF, and could not have come at a worse moment for the *Regia Aeronautica*. After less than a month of war, all of the CR.42 units sent to the desert border area (El Adem and Tobruk T2 airfields) were in the process of being retired from the frontline because of technical problems caused by the sand that had put almost all of their engines out of action. Added to the combat losses of 4 July and the odd aircraft written off on the ground, this meant that only a few CR.42s now remained operational in Libya, namely those of 13° *Gruppo*, which up to that time had been based on the airfields around Tripoli and Benghazi, where concrete runways had protected the aeroplanes from the effects of the sand. 9° *Gruppo*, then based in Italy, was immediately ordered to Libya, arriving on 12 July, while additional attrition replacements were flown in directly from Italy.

However, the pace of action over the front had by then slowed down because the RAF units also had to maintain their strength. The newly arrived Italian aircraft were prudently kept away from the frontline airfields while they were fitted with sand filters prior to being sent into combat.

OVERLEAF
At around 1700 hrs on 8 August 1940 a formation of 13 Gladiators from No. 80 Sqn and a formation of 16 CR.42s of 9° and 10° *Gruppi* clashed over the desert near Gabr Saleh, in Libya. The combat, which started at an altitude of 2,700m (9,000ft), lasted 15 minutes. The Italian formation was slowly climbing from its base at El Adem to reach a patrol area along the frontier with Egypt, and the Gladiators were hunting for the CR.42s. The British pilots were trying out a new formation, with different sub-flights of three (vics) stepped at different heights and maintaining contact through R/T. Tactical command of the formation was given to future ace Flt Lt Thomas Pattle, flying in the highest sub-flight. When he spotted the Italian fighters below, Pattle ordered all the lower sub-flights to attack in sequence. The end result was impressive – eight *Falcos* failed to return, either shot down or obliged to force-land, for the loss of only two Gladiators and a single pilot.

Flt Lt 'Pat' Pattle is seen here at the controls of Gladiator I L8011/YK-O of No. 80 Sqn in 1940. Pattle claimed ten CR.42s destroyed while flying the Gloster fighter, and was the most successful pilot of the type, with 15 victories to his name prior to swapping to the Hurricane in Greece. (Andrew Thomas)

10° *Gruppo* was back in action with 16 fighters on 22 July, joining the few combat-worthy aeroplanes of 13° *Gruppo* at El Adem. The poor results achieved in the first combats involving the CR.42 led to an increase in the size of the Italian formations, which now started to resemble those that had flown over Spain. On 23 July, over Sidi Azeiz, three Gladiators of No. 33 Sqn were surprised by 18 CR.42s of the two *gruppi* and N5774 was shot down. Plt Off Preston escaped by parachute. Two victories were claimed by the Italians, and it seems that the victor over Preston was future ace Tenente Guglielmo Chiarini of 13° *Gruppo*.

The next day No. 33 Sqn put up five Gladiators (more from No. 112 Sqn were also present), and over Bardia they encountered a 17-strong formation of CR.42s. The Italian pilots claimed two victories and the RAF pilots four. In fact both formations lost a single aircraft. Gladiator N5775 was forced-landed by Sgt Shaw, while Capitano Lanfranco of 10° *Gruppo* had to bail out and was made a PoW.

On 25 July, the pilots of No. 33 Sqn experienced their toughest combat to date when five Gladiators of 'B' Flight, reinforced by more from No. 112 Sqn, tried to jump 'seven' CR.42s over Bardia. This time the Italian biplanes (actually only five fighters of 13° *Gruppo*) turned the tables on their opponents. Flg Off P. E. C. Strahan (detached from No. 112 Sqn) had to force-land, while the other pilots of No. 33 Sqn fought for their lives, claiming five CR.42s destroyed and reporting the skill of their opponents. As recounted by author Michel Lavigne in his book *Hurricanes over the Sand*, Plt Off Woodward declared after this combat, 'They were clean fighters those Wops, and quite the equal of any Hun in the skill of combat flying'. He also remembered that he was saved by the Gladiator's ability to out-turn the Fiats at low altitude.

In fact, even if the Operations Record Book (ORB) of No. 33 Sqn did not report any losses, it transpires that a team from No. 51 Repair and Salvage Unit (RSU) moved to Sidi Barrani on 27 July to salvage 'crashed' Gladiators N5768 and L9046 of No. 33 Sqn. They were the aircraft flown by Woodward and fellow ace Flg Off E. H. 'Dixie' Dean, the latter's machine having to be written off. The Italians, who suffered no losses, claimed only one confirmed victory and two probables, by Sergente Rovero Abbarchi, Sergente Maggiore Leone Basso and Tenente Giovanni Beduz, respectively.

These losses were felt by the RAF unit, which was unable to take part in actions on 26 and 27 July, when escorted formations of Italian assault aircraft stopped a penetration by British armoured forces in the Sidi Rezegh area, causing heavy losses to the 11th Hussars. On 28 July No. 33 Sqn was replaced in the frontline by No. 80 Sqn, always supplemented by detachments from No. 112 Sqn.

Although No. 80 Sqn was soon to become the best of all of the Gladiator units, its first encounter with the *Regia Aeronautica* was not an auspicious one. On the afternoon of 4 August a patrol of four of its newly arrived Gladiator Is, aloft to escort a Lysander, was surprised over the border area by six CR.32s of 160ᵃ *Squadriglia*, which shot down L8009, flown by Flg Off P. G. Wykeham-Barnes (who had shot down two CR.42s in June) and K7908, killing Sgt K. G. R. Rew. A third Gladiator, K7923, flown by Plt Off J. H. Lancaster, was heavily damaged and its pilot wounded.

At about the same time a huge formation of CR.42s from 9° and 10° *Gruppi*, which had clashed with Gladiators of No. 112 Sqn whilst they were escorting Blenheims, was returning to base when it came upon K7910, flown by Flt Lt M. T. StJ. Pattle – the No. 80 Sqn formation leader and sole survivor of the unlucky patrol. Attacked from multiple directions by as many as 'a dozen CR.42s', he too was shot down, but escaped by parachute. No losses were suffered by the *Regia Aeronautica* on this occasion, even though Pattle claimed a Fiat destroyed. There are no details of the part played by the Gladiators of No. 112 Sqn in the aforementioned combat, the records of the unit for this period having been lost. However, it is known that the *Falco* pilots claimed as many as four Gladiators (including Pattle), and that a salvage party of No. 51 RSU reached Sidi Barrani on 6 August to repair L8131 and L7895 of No. 112 Sqn.

At this stage, with the RAF suffering at least 11 Gladiators lost or heavily damaged in two weeks in exchange for a single *Falco*, and air superiority seemingly destined to pass firmly to the Italians, No. 80 Sqn reacted.

On 8 August 13 Gladiators, led by Sqn Ldr Patrick Dunn and Flt Lt Pattle, ambushed a mixed formation of 16 *Falcos* from 9° and 10° *Gruppi* led by Maggiore Carlo Romagnoli. The Gladiator pilots jumped their opponents from the classic 'six o'clock high' position and, after a devastating firing pass during which three Italian fighters were immediately shot down and the rest of the formation was badly disorganised, engaged in a low-level dogfight with their less-manoeuvrable opponents. In the words of Carlo Romagnoli, 'The attack of the Gladiators was the deadliest I have ever seen in my combat career, but the reaction of my men was miraculously immediate'.

Radio control of the RAF formation had been critical in securing the initial surprise, and the Gladiator's superior horizontal manoeuvrability then cost the Italians five more losses. Flg Off V. A. J. Stuckey recorded, 'With trimming gear slightly back, I found I could easily outmanoeuvre aircraft attacking from the rear. No blacking out'. In Flg Off S. Linnard's words, 'No difficulties in keeping astern of enemy aircraft. Enemy invariably looped for evasive action'. In the end, half of the Italian formation failed to return. Maresciallo Norino Renzi was killed in action, Sergenti Enrico Dallari, Aldo Rosa and Sergente Maggiore Antonio Valle bailed out and Sottotenente Alvaro Querci, Sergenti Santo Gino and Lido Poli and Tenente

CR.42 MM4306/91-6 of Tenente Enzo Martissa of 91ᵃ *Squadriglia*, 10° *Gruppo* is recovered by Italian Army troops following his forced landing after sustaining combat damage fighting No. 80 Sqn Gladiators on 8 August 1940. (Enzo Martissa)

ENGAGING THE ENEMY

The San Giorgio Type B reflector gunsight was standard equipment on all Italian fighters, except when it was occasionally replaced by an older ring-and-bead sight. It comprised an optical system with an objective lens of 60mm diameter that projected two light rings and three dots. To aim the guns for a deflection shot, the pilot had to turn on the gunsight and estimate the target's speed and direction. He then had two options. If the component of the target speed orthogonal to the aiming line was around 200km/h, he had to use the smaller ring. If it was around 400km/h he had to use the bigger ring. In both cases he had to open fire when the centre of the target crossed the circumference of the ring. The dots were useful to estimate distance and avoid opening fire at excessive range.

Enzo Martissa force-landed, the last two being severely wounded, although their aeroplanes were later recovered.

The remaining Italian pilots claimed five victories, shooting down the machines of Flt Sgt T. M. Vaughan (K7903), who was killed, and Flt Lt R. V. Evers-Swindell (L8010), and severely damaging the engine of K8011, piloted by Flg Off Wanklyn Flower, who was forced to withdraw.

It was an outstanding victory. An indication of the degree of control that the RAF pilots were able to maintain throughout the encounter is the remarkable accuracy of their claims. Only ten were submitted at the end of the swirling combat – two each for Dunn, Pattle and Linnard, one each for Wykeham-Barnes, Flg Off G. F. Graham, Plt Off Stuckey and the missing Vaughan. Later, the total was increased to 16, perhaps for propaganda purposes. This air battle redressed the balance of the air war to an even match, and practically brought to an end fighter combat between Gladiators and *Falcos* over the Libyan front for almost three months.

When *Falcos* and Gladiators met again, on 31 October 1940, No. 33 Sqn had finally converted to Hurricanes. On that day a formation of 26 SM.79s raided Mersa Matruh and were intercepted by the Gladiators of No. 112 Sqn (at least nine) and 12 Hurricanes of No. 33 Sqn that were defending the base. The bombers were indirectly escorted by 37 CR.42s of the crack 13° *Gruppo* and the recently arrived 151° *Gruppo*. The Italian fighter pilots took good advantage of their height and numbers, falling on the lower RAF fighters or intercepting them while their pilots were concentrating on the Savoias. Ten victories (five for each *gruppo*) were claimed, while the Gladiator pilots were credited with six victories and their counterparts flying Hurricanes four. In reality only the CR.42 of Tenente Gianfranco Perversi was downed, the pilot losing his life.

Hardworking No. 3 Sqn RAAF riggers and fitters stop for a break while overhauling a Gladiator at Gerawla, in Egypt, in November 1940. (Doug Norrie)

On 19 November 1940 No. 3 Sqn RAAF encountered Italian fighters for the first time when four Gladiators were intercepted by six CR.42s of 82ª *Squadriglia*, 13° *Gruppo*. In the ensuing combat, which reportedly lasted 25 minutes, Sqn Ldr P. R. Heath, in Gladiator N5750, was shot down and killed. Heath's crash site was discovered on 13 December about a mile from Sidi Barrani. A bullet hole was found in his oxygen mask, so he was possibly dead before he crashed. He was buried next to his destroyed aircraft. (Doug Norrie)

In fact the British fighter pilots, who had claimed three victories over *Falcos*, lost seven of their number – five Gladiators and two Hurricanes, plus another Hurricane severely damaged. Almost all of the Gladiator losses were credited by the RAF pilots to other causes rather than to the action of the Italian fighters. Plt Off B. B. E. Duff was the only one positively credited to the Fiats. Plt Off R. A. Acworth and 2Lt E. R. Smith reportedly collided in mid-air during the combat, Flt Lt G. Schwab suffered engine trouble and was obliged to force-land (perhaps in K8054, later passed to the *EVA*) and Flg Off R. H. Clarke was last seen chasing some SM.79s, and his demise was credited to their return fire.

However, from the reports of the returning Italian pilots it seems that Sergente Maggiore Roberto Marchi of 151° *Gruppo* finished off Plt Off Duff after he was attacked by the whole of 366ª *Squadriglia*, Schwab was claimed by Capitano Domenico Bevilacqua of 13° *Gruppo* and Clarke almost certainly fell victim to Capitano Bruno Locatelli, the CO of 368ª *Squadriglia*, who reported that his claimed Gladiator exploded in mid-air. Finally, Tenente Gianfranco Perversi was seen to chase two British fighters and collide with one of them after having shot down the other – a situation closely matching the reported collision between Acworth and Smith. Whatever the truth, the combat was a blow for the RAF fighters, and showed that the CR.42 had a definite edge in performance over the Gladiator at heights above 10,000ft.

In mid-November No. 3 Sqn RAAF reached the frontline, and on the 19th of the month four of the 'green' Australians performed a reconnaissance and were intercepted at low level by six CR.42s of 13° *Gruppo*, which were part of a stronger formation that was strafing British troops in the area. A confused dogfight started, with much over-claiming on both sides, but 13° *Gruppo* again came off best. Led by Tenente Guglielmo Chiarini, the Italians claimed six confirmed victories. They had in fact shot down N5750, flown by Sqn Ldr P. R. Heath (who was killed), and heavily damaged N5753, flown by Flt Lt B. R. Pelly, who was obliged to force-land at Minquar Quaim advanced airstrip. The Australians were no less optimistic, claiming four victories when four CR.42s were only slightly damaged.

The next day brought revenge, six Gladiators of No. 112 Sqn being ordered to cover a formation of nine Hurricanes from No. 33 Sqn that were in turn tasked with escorting some Lysanders. The Hurricanes were engaged by an 18-strong formation of 9° *Gruppo* east of Sidi Barrani, and while they were sparring with them the Gladiator pilots took the opportunity to dive over part of the Italian formation, claiming eight Fiats for no recorded losses. Three Italian fighters failed to return, Sergente Franceso Putzu and Sottotenente Carlo Agnelli being killed, while Tenente Aldo Gon forced-landed and rejoined the Italian lines on foot. Four more fighters were damaged.

In return, 9° *Gruppo* claimed four Gladiators among seven victories. Even though no Gloster fighters were recorded as lost by the RAF, it is worth pointing out that, while describing this successful combat, Plt Off Acworth remembered that 'seven aircraft had been shot down in the engagement, and all the Gladiator pilots had survived the fight, although two had made forced landings'. One of them, possibly K6142, was salvaged by No. 51 RSU on 27 November.

No more actions were fought between Gladiators and CR.42s until the *Compass* offensive started on 9 December 1940. By that time the backbone of the RAF fighter force in theatre was the Hurricane, but Gladiators remained in service with Nos. 112 and 3 Sqns because there were not enough Hawker fighters with which to re-equip them. Very little is known of the activities of the former unit during this period, but No. 3 Sqn RAAF saw combat against the Italian biplanes quite frequently, performing daily patrols with small formations from advanced landing strips. In fact the unit was the last one to engage the *Falco* in combat in this sector.

On the afternoon of 10 December the RAAF fought a very successful action over the frontline in the region of Sidi Barrani. A large formation of 151° *Gruppo* aircraft was ground strafing, wisely keeping two-thirds of its aircraft at greater altitude to cover the others. The weather deteriorated and it became impossible to maintain visual contact between the *squadriglia* that was strafing and the other two, so, taking full advantage of this otherwise unfavourable situation, four Australian Gladiators led by the unit's CO, Sqn Ldr I. D. McLachlan, jumped the strafing Italian fighters, McLachlan shooting down the Fiat of Sergente Gino Bogoni, who was made a PoW. Other Gladiator pilots damaged three more, two of which were recorded as possibles and later confirmed. No claims were submitted by the Italians.

Flg Off Peter Turnbull of No. 3 Sqn RAAF is sitting in Gladiator II L9044/NW-Z *Sweet Sue* at Gerawla circa November 1940. This aircraft was one of 18 Gladiator IIs that had originally been delivered to the Royal Egyptian Air Force. Turnbull was flying L9044 when he damaged a Fiat G.50bis on 25 January 1941. (Doug Norrie)

CR.42s of 73ª *Squadriglia*, 9° *Gruppo* at El Adem in 1940. Again, rocks liberally cover the advanced landing ground. (Oblach, via Fulvio Chianese)

On 12 December five Gladiators of No. 3 Sqn RAAF met 18 Fiats of 9° and 10° *Gruppi* and again claimed three without loss, despite two Italian claims. Sergente Onorino Crestani failed to return. During this combat Flg Off A. H. Boyd claimed his fourth CR.42.

The promising progress of No. 3 Sqn RAAF came to an abrupt end the following morning when six Gladiators intercepted five SM.79s over Sollum. The young Australians made for the bombers without taking care to cover their backs, and were jumped by the ten-strong Fiat escort provided by 9° *Gruppo*, led by Capitano Antonio Larsimont-Pergameni. Consequently, N5765 was lost and its pilot, Flt Lt C. B. Gaden, killed, Flg Offs L. D. A. Winten and W. S. Arthur had to bail out, the latter after being rammed by Larsimont himself, and two more aeroplanes crash-landed. In one of them Boyd had claimed two additional CR.42s. In fact, apart from the damage suffered by the aircraft flown by Larsimont, who had collided with Gladiator N5752 after misjudging the distance while firing at it from dead astern, the Italians suffered no losses. Three Fiats were damaged, however. Larsimont reached the advanced airfield at Menastir but had to abandon his aircraft there because of the imminent arrival of British troops.

Operations by the advanced detachment practically ceased until new aeroplanes could arrive from No. 3 Sqn's base at Gerawla, but the Australians stubbornly continued to take off in their two remaining fighters, joining formations put up by No. 112 Sqn.

More Gladiators arrived on 18 December, but the era of the patrols over the front had ended for No. 3 Sqn RAAF, its fighters being mainly tasked with escorting artillery-spotting aircraft. It was in this role that the aggressive Australians had their last combat with the CR.42s when, over Sollum during the morning of 26 December 1940, eight Gladiators diverted from their task of escorting a Lysander to try to intercept ten SM.79s seen above, with a huge escort of CR.42s.

The interception did not materialise owing to the intervention of the 31-strong escort, but in the ensuing dogfight the Australians claimed two confirmed victories. Flg Off W. S. Arthur and Flt Lt G. H. Steege had managed to shoot down the aircraft of Capitano Guido Bobba, CO of 74ª *Squadriglia*, 23° *Gruppo*, which had just arrived from Sicily. Bobba, who was listed as missing in action, was also credited with one victory during this combat, making him an ace. Two more Italian pilots claimed victories, but the Australians admitted only to slight damage to three aircraft. The damage suffered was perhaps not so slight, as this was the last combat of the year for the Australians. Indeed, on 31 December a salvage team from No. 51 RSU arrived at Sollum to salvage two of the unit's Gladiators. One of those machines was almost certainly the mount of Plt Off John Jackson, who noted after this action:

My first fight on the patrol this afternoon, eight of us on the job seeing ten bombers and goodness knows how many fighters up above us over Sollum Bay at about 15,000 to 18,000ft. We went straight for them and I got into the middle of about a dozen at 17,000ft but couldn't get a decent shot – fired 350 rounds but my fuselage guns were not working. Had my aeroplane badly shot about. One bullet grazed my parachute straps and bruised my shoulder, a couple more whistled past my head and tore the cockpit cover edges, breaking the glass, a few more tore a lot of the fabric off the starboard wings and a few more went through the lower mainplanes. Thanks to providence, I didn't get hit – the blighter must have had a good shot at me. There were too many of them for me to get a go at any one – quite a thrilling experience. Alan Rawlinson reckons he got one, also Jock Perrin, and there were three other possibles. Not bad work seeing how outnumbered we were. A few of the others also collected an

Gladiator K6142 of No. 3 Sqn RAAF is recovered after a takeoff accident at Gerawla on 31 December 1940. The fighter's engine cut shortly after Flg Off John Jackson had taken off, and he could not avoid running into a wadi. The pilot was unharmed, but the aircraft turned up on its nose and was considered beyond repair. K6142 had previously served with No. 112 Sqn, and it was struck off charge on 27 January 1941. Jackson later became an ace, with seven victories to his name. (Doug Norrie)

odd bullet hole. It's a pity we haven't got better aircraft, as the Gladiators are nowhere near as good as the CR.42s. Our air strength is about a tenth of theirs.

The combat of 26 December 1940 marked an end to the six months of confrontation between Gladiators and CR.42s over North Africa.

EAST AFRICA

Gladiators and CR.42s clashed over this front for the first time on 2 July 1940 after British forces in Aden had initiated a series of attacks to neutralise the Italian airfield at Assab, in Abyssinia. In an effort to protect the base six fighters had been hastily flown in, and they were to constitute the new 414ª *Squadriglia*. In the early morning of the 2nd, three Gladiators of No. 94 Sqn, led by unit CO, Sqn Ldr W. T. F. Wightman, attacked the airfield. Some of the Italian fighters tried to scramble but were caught by the Gladiators when they had barely left the ground. Two CR.42s were claimed shot down and one more destroyed on the ground. Sergente Luigi Barengo was killed and Sergente Fosco Celleri bailed out, and the CR.42 destroyed on the ground was also confirmed by Italian sources.

On 10 July No. 94 Sqn was again over Assab, this time destroying the last three CR.42s of 414ª *Squadriglia* on the ground. The unit was consequently disbanded, while the airfield at Assab was abandoned. It is often reported that the first loss of a Gladiator in the sector came two days later, on 13 July, when L9042 of No. 94 Sqn was intercepted by fighters of 413ª *Squadriglia* and shot down south of Assab, with the death of Plt Off Carter, but Italian documents suggest that he was shot down by anti-aircraft fire. It was not until 8 August that the Italian fighters were able partly to avenge the losses suffered at Assab. That morning two CR.32s and a 413ª *Squadriglia* CR.42 piloted by Sottotenente Miroslav Komjanc flew over Berbera and destroyed N2284 and N5890 on the ground, these two No. 94 Sqn Gladiators having detached

This Gladiator of No. 1 Sqn SAAF had previously served with No. 80 Sqn, as it still carries that unit's pre-war 'OD' codes. (SAAF Museum)

there to defend the city. No more fighters were subsequently based at this very exposed airfield prior to the city falling into Italian hands on 19 August 1940.

Shortly thereafter a flight of Gladiators from No. 1 Sqn SAAF was sent to Sudan to reinforce 'K' Flight, and the South Africans now started to appear over the frontline. Documents from Italian fighter units in-theatre were lost at the end of the campaign, and the records of No. 1 Sqn SAAF are incomplete, lacking accounts of activities for weeks at a time, or having them only roughly drafted. One loose paper from the South African unit describes an encounter over the Sudanese town of Kassala in September between three Gladiators led by Capt S. van Schalkwyk and an unknown number of Italian fighters. Two victories were claimed by the South Africans, but this action does not appear in any Italian documentation, and the nature of the South African document describing it leaves doubt that perhaps it did not happen at all!

The first encounter in Sudan between Gladiators and CR.42s that is corroborated by documentary evidence occurred on 4 October 1940 over the border town of Metemma. That day three Gladiator pilots met a reported three CR.42s of 412ª *Squadriglia* and claimed two victories. In fact the fighter flown by Sergente Ottavio Bracci was shot down, the wounded pilot being forced to take to his parachute. In return, Sottotenente Fiorindo Rosmino claimed one victory unconfirmed, No. 1 Sqn SAAF recording that Capt B. J. L. Boyle's aeroplane was damaged.

On 16 October seven CR.42s of 412ª *Squadriglia*, led by the unit's CO, Capitano Antonio Raffi, attacked the airstrip at Gedaref, destroying eight Wellesleys of No. 47 Sqn on the ground. While leading his aeroplanes down to strafe, Raffi discovered two 'Gladiators' that were trying to take off. He was over them before they were able to leave the ground, and claimed both destroyed. However, his first claims for Gladiators were actually two Vickers Vincents of No. 430 Flight, which went up in flames.

During the afternoon of 18 October No. 1 Sqn SAAF retaliated against 412ª *Squadriglia's* advanced landing ground at Barentu when Capt Boyle and Lts A. Duncan and R. Pare destroyed three CR.42s on the ground in a surprise attack. The next encounter between the two units was over the same area on 4 November. On that day

A war-weary SAAF Gladiator I somewhere in East Africa in 1940-41. Note the sheer size of the fighter's Watts wooden two-blade propeller. (SAAF Museum)

A Gladiator II of No. 1 Sqn SAAF at the Wajir detachment in Kenya. This is probably N5856 *Lulu Belle*, which later served with No. 2 Sqn SAAF and No. 237 'Rhodesia' Sqn, before being struck off charge on 1 May 1943. Note the aircraft spotter in the tree behind the Gladiator – the only form of early warning 'equipment' in-theatre. (SAAF Museum)

the South Africans claimed three confirmed victories against a formation of three or four Fiats, Capt Boyle again being credited with a victory. They had in fact shot down the fighter flown by Sottotenente Mario Proserpio, who was wounded. An unknown Italian pilot claimed one confirmed victory and Sergente Maggiore Luigi Baron one probable, although the South Africans again did not report any losses.

On the morning of 6 November 1940 the first offensive of the war by Commonwealth forces started when an Indian brigade tried to re-take the Sudanese border town of Gallabat and nearby Metemma. Gladiators from both 'K' Flight and No. 1 Sqn SAAF covered the action, patrolling over the assaulting troops from the outset. 412ᵃ *Squadriglia* reacted strongly to this attack. In the early hours of the

morning six *Falcos* led by Capitano Antonio Raffi jumped three Gladiators of 'K' Flight, shooting them all down. The unit's CO, Flt Lt K. H. Savage, lost his life in L7614, Plt Off Kirk bailed out of K7969 and Plt Off J. Hamlyn forced-landed in L7612. They were the victims, respectively, of Raffi himself, Tenente Niso Provinciali and Sergente Pietro Morlotti.

A short while later the South Africans arrived in the area, where they too were met by the patrolling Fiats. Raffi shot down and killed Maj van Schalkwyk, while Sottotenente Rosmino claimed Capt Boyle in N5852. In just one hour the assaulting troops had been left without any fighter cover, and colonial Italian Caproni Ca.133s started to bomb and strafe at will.

In the afternoon the remaining Commonwealth fighters – four Gladiators of No. 1 Sqn SAAF and the last Gloster fighter from 'K' Flight – tried again to cover their troops. The South Africans were successful in shooting down two Capronis, but again the Fiats of 412ª *Squadriglia* exacted their toll, shooting down K7977 (the single surviving machine of 'K' Flight) and killing its pilot, Flg Off Jack Maurice Hayward. This time the Italians claimed two victories, and it is possible that at least one of them was submitted by Tenente Mario Visintini. The South Africans also claimed two victories, but there were no Italian losses.

Within two days of the offensive commencing Commonwealth troops were forced to leave the battlefield by the combined effort of the Italian bombers and the counterattacking colonial infantry. Encounters over Metemma continued in the following days, the Italians claiming another Gladiator on the 11th, but this was not confirmed by SAAF documents. On 13 November the Gladiators returned to Khartoum.

The next encounter between the two types came on 27 December 1940 when a detachment from 412ª *Squadriglia* that had taken off from Gondar strafed Gedaref airfield. The Fiat pilots did not find suitable targets, however, as there was just one aircraft on the airfield. They were then intercepted at low level by five Gladiators and Lt T. Condon shot down Sottotenente Filippo Sola, who was killed. The Italian pilots in turn claimed four victories, two of them being credited to Sergente Maggiore Enzo

Capt Brian Boyle of No. 1 Sqn SAAF in front of Gladiator N5852. Boyle claimed two CR.42s flying this aircraft before being shot down by a *Falco* on 6 November 1940. He later downed a third CR.42 while flying Gladiators, then claimed two additional kills in Hurricanes, giving him a total of five victories. (SAAF Museum)

Omiccioli for his sixth and seventh victories (not all of his previous successes were individual ones). Omiccioli stated that one of his opponents forced-landed while the other went down in flames, but the South Africans reported only slight damage to N5789.

On 12 January 1941 two Gladiators were over the border town of Aroma, in Sudan, when they discovered a pair of SM.79s and carried out a stern attack. Three CR.42s were flying above the Savoias, and in the words of Lt Theron:

> One out of a formation of three CR.42s flying at approximately 15,000ft dived down and fired a short burst at Lt Warren, the CR.42 then continuing its dive and disappearing. Both Gladiators dived and levelled out at about 20ft. Two minutes later Lt J. S. R. Warren's aircraft caught fire and crashed. The pilot was killed and the aircraft completely burnt out.

This rare account is interesting because it describes clearly the tactics that the CR.42 pilots were using to prevail over their more manoeuvrable opponents. After the war Antonio Raffi recorded, 'The Gloster was a dangerous aeroplane for the CR.42 pilot if he manoeuvred below 3,000m [10,000ft]. Above that height the CR.42, being equipped with a supercharger, was definitely superior'. In the words of Capitano Ricci, CO of 410ª *Squadriglia* equipped with CR.32s, 'The Gloster Gladiator fighter was very dangerous because of its good armament and great manoeuvrability'. The counter to this manoeuvrability was hit-and-run attacks, as Vivian Voss, the Intelligence Officer of No. 1 Sqn SAAF remembered:

> One of the first things new pilots were taught was to develop the rubber neck. Failing this, they were certain sooner or later to be jumped. When Lt J. Van der Merwe first joined the squadron he could not believe that the rubber neck was really necessary. It was not long before two CR.42s, coming down on his tail like arrows from heaven, cured him once and for all of his casual views on keeping a watch for fighters. He was one of the lucky ones to survive such an attack.

On the other hand, the engagement of 27 December had demonstrated once again that at low altitude the Gladiator was at least as deadly as the CR.42, if not more so.

The start of the British offensive over Eritrea in early 1941 brought No. 1 Sqn SAAF an increasing complement of Hurricanes, and also an increase in air combat. On 24 and 26 January the Italians claimed three Gladiators and the South African Gladiator pilots one probable

This photograph of Sergente Maggiore Luigi Baron of 412ª *Squadriglia* was taken after the war, when he was a flight instructor at Lecce Flying School. Baron served in East Africa, where he claimed 12 victories while flying the CR.42, four of them Gladiators. On 25 March 1941 he claimed a Hurricane over Keren, before being shot down himself and wounded, probably by Lt Robin Pare of No. 1 Sqn SAAF. Baron escaped from hospital and hid from British forces for two years. In 1943 he was able to embark on the *Duilio*, a ship used for the repatriation of civilians, bound for Italy, with a false identity and false papers that stated he was mentally ill. (Rossella Baron)

CR.42. No losses were recorded on either side, however. On 29 January a mixed formation of five Gladiators and eight Hurricanes caught three CR.42s defending their base at Gura. The ensuing combat was fought at medium to low altitude, and this time the Fiats were able to escape – Capitano Raffi recorded that he took ten bullets in his parachute and lost the fabric on the fuselage close to the cockpit, as well as on the tailplane. In return, his gunfire damaged N5851, flown by Lt H. P. Smith, who landed unhurt.

The Italians were not so lucky on 3 February, when five Gladiators attacked the airfield at Gondar. Two of the three Italian fighters on standby took off and flew in the wrong direction, leaving just a solitary Fiat at Gondar when the Gladiators arrived at very low altitude over the airstrip. Sergente Maggiore Enzo Omiccioli scrambled alone, and according to eyewitnesses on the ground he was surrounded by the whole SAAF formation and hit by two Gladiators while he was firing on a third. The ace fell from 200m (650ft) and was killed, having fallen victim to Capt Boyle. Omiccioli's own gunfire had probably hit N5831, which crashed on landing at Azozo. The brave Omiccioli, who had taken off even though his comrades, on seeing the five Gladiators, had asked him to take cover, was granted a posthumous *Medaglia d'oro al Valor Militare*.

More and more Hurricanes were arriving for No. 1 Sqn SAAF, and the Gladiators were relegated to second-line duties. Their last combat claim was on 5 February, when two, together with four Hurricanes, tangled with a reported six CR.42s over Asmara. Two of the Italian fighters were shot down, Sottotenente Giovanni Consoli losing his life in one of them. Two victories were claimed by Hurricane pilots and one by Gladiator pilot Lt T. Condon.

When, in mid-February, the British offensive was stopped on the slopes of the mountains around the Eritrean town of Keren, the *Regia Aeronautica* had been practically wiped out. The Italian HQ decided to stop flying missions over the front and conserve its remaining strength to counter the final British offensive. Meanwhile, the maximum possible number of CR.42s was sent from Italy so that when Commonwealth troops attacked again on 15 March the *Regia Aeronautica* had 12 CR.42s defending the Northern Front.

In the meantime some Gladiators that had been relinquished by No. 1 Sqn SAAF had been given to No. 237 'Rhodesia' Sqn, a ground-attack unit that had operated with great distinction flying the Hawker Hardy. On Christmas Eve 1940 one of the unit's Hardies had claimed a Ca.133, and its crew had celebrated the event with this short rhyme:

Happy Christmas unto thee,
We have downed a one-three-three.
If we only get our due,
We shall down a forty-two.

Shortly after the offensive had started on 16 March, No. 237 'Rhodesia' Sqn's Plt Off P. H. S. Simmonds was busy strafing Italian troops in Keren in one of the recently allocated Gladiators when he was attacked by a Fiat.

Sottotenente Ildebrando Malavolta takes off in CR.42 MM7117 on 24 October 1941 for his last mission. Lt L. C. H. Hope, in Gladiator 1346, subsequently caught Malavolta by surprise at low altitude over Digna and shot him down. (Roberto Gentilli)

Quickly turning the tables on his opponent, he shot down Sottotenente Eugenio Rella of 412ª *Squadriglia* – the Italian pilot was killed. The Christmas rhyme had been prophetic.

The *Regia Aeronautica's* remaining fighters reacted at full strength against the British offensive, with more experienced pilots such as Maresciallo Aroldo Soffritti and Sergente Maggiore Luigi Baron regularly taking off twice a day. 412ª *Squadriglia's* swansong came on 18 March. In the early morning four CR.42s attacked the airfield at Agordat, destroying a Wellesley and badly damaging two Hurricanes on the ground. Later, four CR.42 pilots bounced three Gladiators of 'K' Flight over Keren, claiming four badly hit, later upgraded to shot down – one of the claims was probably attributable to Baron. The day ended with the shooting down of a Hardy of No. 237 Sqn.

The 'K' Flight records for March are missing, and those of No. 203 Group record a single Gladiator damaged before the formation turned back to base. That same day a salvage party from No. 52 RSU arrived at the satellite landing ground of Agordat to inspect two Gladiators that had force-landed there and had to be dismantled and sent back to Khartoum by truck, thus partly confirming the Italian claims.

On 22 March 'K' Flight left for Egypt, and the remaining Italian fighters were duly slaughtered by the Hurricanes. Two of the best pilots, Baron and Pietro Morlotti, were shot down on the 25th, the latter being killed. Keren fell on the 27th, followed by Addis Ababa on 5 April. The British advance into Ethiopian territory continued steadily, and by the end of July the remaining Italian troops had retreated to Gondar. With them were three CR.42s (MM7117, MM7118 and MM4403). Only two of these remained airworthy when the last combat between Gladiators and CR.42s took place on the afternoon of 24 October.

On that day Sottotenente Ildebrando Malavolta was ordered to reconnoitre a bridge near the Kulkaber Pass. As he arrived over the target, the No. 3 Sqn SAAF detachment based on the Dabat Landing Ground scrambled two Gladiators. Lt L. C. H. Hope in Gladiator 1346 caught Malavolta by surprise at low altitude over Digna and shot him down, the Italian perishing when his fighter, MM7117, crashed and

CR.42s of 365ª *Squadriglia*, 150º *Gruppo* undergo maintenance at Gjirokastër, in Albania, in 1940. (Roberto Gentilli)

burst into flames at 1745 hrs. Hope recorded in his combat report, 'I wish to pay tribute to the pilot of the '42 – he was a brave man', and on the morning of 25 October he dropped this message over Malavolta's Gondar base – 'Tribute to the pilot of the Fiat. He was a brave man. South African Air Force'. Ildebrando Malavolta was granted a posthumous *Medaglia d'oro al Valor Militare.*

GREECE

Operations over Greece by No. 80 Sqn started on 19 November 1940. It was not a moment too soon, as the *EVA*, after three weeks of effective operations at a sustained pace, was now collapsing.

At around midday nine Gladiators of 'B' Flight, led by Flt Lt Pattle, carried out a patrol over the frontline, led by three PZLs of 21 *Mira*. The Gladiators flew over Korçë, where many Italian fighters were seen and engaged. After a low-altitude dogfight nine victories were claimed. That day four CR.42s of 160° *Gruppo*, led by Tenente Torquato Testerini, were returning to base after an uneventful patrol. It was a small formation because the tactics in the opening phase of the Greek campaign were to use small numbers of aircraft so as to be able to maintain a continuous protective umbrella over the Italian troops they were supporting. The CR.42s were reportedly attacked by 20 Gladiators and three PZLs, and Sergente Maggiore Natale Viola was killed in MM6996, possibly falling victim to Pattle – he achieved ace status during the combat.

News of the combat arrived in Korçë, whereupon the eight remaining serviceable aeroplanes were scrambled by Capitano Paolo Arcangeletti against '20 Glosters and three PZLs orbiting over the base that had already attacked one of our patrols'. The Gladiators fell like hawks on the climbing CR.42s and two more were shot down, killing Maresciallo Giuseppe Salvadori and Sergente Maggiore Arturo Bonato. A victory was claimed by Sergente Maggiore Luciano Tarantini and a probable by Capitano Arcangeletti. One or perhaps both of them had attacked Plt Off V. A. J. Stuckey, who had also become an ace that day, and he was badly shot up and wounded. The Italians also lost a G.50 of *Gruppo Autonomo Berat*, and a fourth CR.42 was badly damaged and its pilot, Sergente Maggiore Walter Ratticchieri, wounded. This trouncing impressed the Italians, who decided that the use of small fighter formations over the frontline should be discontinued.

On the morning 27 November Capitano Nicola Magaldi took off from Vlorë at the head of eight fighters from 150° *Gruppo*. During the mission Magaldi spotted some bombers and, while investigating them with his section, lost touch with the rest of his formation. The three CR.42s were found and bounced over Ioannina by nine Gladiators of No. 80 Sqn on an offensive patrol. Magaldi was killed and Sergente

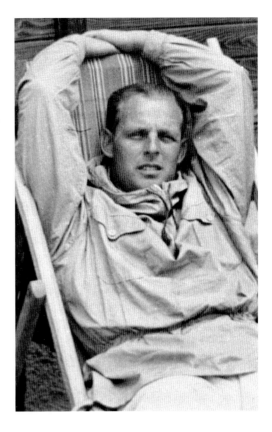

Capitano Giorgio Graffer relaxes in a mountain suit some years before the war. Graffer is often credited with five individual victories, but these claims are difficult to verify in *Regia Aeronautica* documentation. The latter reveals only a single individual victory, claimed for a ramming attack that Graffer carried out alone against an Armstrong Whitworth Whitley bomber over Turin, and 11 shared victories credited to him while he was fighting in formation with other aircraft of his *gruppo*. However, it seems possible that four of these shared victories were individual ones, credited as shared in accordance with the policy usually followed by the unit's CO, Colonello Arrigo Tessari. (Roberto Gentilli)

Negri, wounded in one leg, landed a heavily damaged aircraft at 1500 hrs. They were victims of Flt Lt E. G. Jones and Sgt D. S. Gregory.

The loss of Magaldi, who was granted a posthumous *Medaglia d'oro al Valor Militare* for bravery, was a hard blow for 150° *Gruppo*, which decided to seek immediate revenge. At 0845 hrs the following day Capitano Giorgio Graffer took off at the head of nine more fighters from the *gruppo* to seek out the Gladiators. Twenty-eight-year-old Graffer was a prominent personality in his unit, and having already claimed many victories, he was without question the leading fighter pilot of the *Regia Aeronautica* in Greece.

Twenty minutes after takeoff Graffer sighted a vic of three Gladiators below him, and he immediately dived to attack them. It was a trap. Three miles behind this trio were another three RAF biplanes, and then three more. Summoned by radio, these fighters were able to surprise the Italian formation intent on bouncing its presumed victims. Graffer was killed, Sergente Corrado Mignani was seen to collide with a Gladiator and was also lost and Sergente Tommaso Pacini was shot down – he was subsequently driven back to his unit in an army truck, suffering from shock. Additionally, Maresciallo Guglielmo Bacci and Sergente Zotti were wounded, although they were able to return to base.

One Gladiator was lost, Flg Off H. U. Sykes in N5812 being killed when he collided with Mignani. Gladiators N5816, N5854, N5788 and N5786 were reported damaged, the first two heavily, and Flt Lt Jones was wounded after claiming two CR.42s. For the Italians, however, it had been the heaviest blow suffered since the beginning of the campaign. Graffer received a posthumous *Medaglia d'oro al Valor Militare*.

On 2 December the Greeks received their first Gladiators, and more arrived two days later. Four machines from No. 112 Sqn joined No. 80 Sqn on temporary attachment, and they took off with ten other aeroplanes on 4 December to sweep the frontline. Here they met 15 CR.42s of 150° *Gruppo*, led by the CO, Tenente Colonello Rolando Pratelli. While flying at an altitude of 4,500m (14,700ft), Pratelli saw a group of three Gladiators slightly lower than him and off to his right. He immediately dived to attack, but while doing so he discovered, some 1,000m (3,300ft) higher, two additional formations of Gladiators, each estimated at ten aircraft strong.

Once again it was No. 80 Sqn, carrying out its tried and tested tactic that had served the unit well since the previous August. One small formation acted as bait for the enemy fighters by flying lower, with the rest of the Gladiators above, ready to intervene. This time Pratelli was partly able to save the day. Knowing that ten Fiat G.50s of 154° *Gruppo*, led by Maggiore Angelo Mastragostino, were supposed to be cruising at a higher altitude than his CR.42s, he pulled out of the dive and started climbing towards the Fiats. Meanwhile, the higher Gladiators had arrived, not totally unnoticed, and the usual wild dogfight ensued. Mastragostino finally saw what was happening below, and his *Freccias* joined the combat.

Only 13 CR.42s landed back at Vlorë, their pilots claiming two Gladiators shot down and two more as probables, while an additional fighter was credited to the pilots of 154° *Gruppo*, which did not suffer any losses. British pilots claimed eight *Falcos* and a G.50. Both Tenente Alberto Triolo and Sottotenente Paolo Penna were reported missing in action and five more Fiats were damaged. The No. 80 Sqn ORB listed no losses, but the No. 112 Sqn pilots duly noted 'Three casualties in our formation', one of whom was the CO, Sqn Ldr W. J. Hickey, shot down in N5859. He probably fell victim of the *Falcos*, as he was seen hard pressed by them by Pattle, who himself claimed three CR.42s.

Finally, on 21 December, Gladiators and CR.42s clashed for the fifth time. Ten RAF fighters, again led by Hickey, tried to intercept some Cant Z.1007bis bombers and were counterattacked by the Italian escort, comprising 21 *Falcos* of 150° and 160° *Gruppi*. After a swirling dogfight the Italians submitted claims for ten victories, while losing three aircraft and two pilots (Tenenti Mario Carancini and Mario Frascadore). No. 80 Sqn claimed eight victories and suffered two losses (Hickey and Flg Off A. D. Ripley, who were killed in N5816 and N5854, respectively). Additionally, N5834 and N5854 were badly damaged and their pilots wounded. Pattle, who claimed one victory, reported:

> I was forced to use continuous evasive action against the repeated attacks of the '42s in quick succession. After each attack the enemy would climb for height while another would dive down to attack. In this way I was unable to climb up to their height as continuous evasive actions made climbing impossible. For fully five minutes I was kept on the defensive without being able to fire a single shot in return.

The Italians were clearly using the dive-and-zoom tactics already reported by the SAAF in East Africa.

The following morning only four of the twenty Gladiators in-theatre remained serviceable at the unit's Lárisa base, and despite the strenuous efforts of the groundcrews, who managed to make five more available before evening, the unit was replaced by 21 *Mira* on 23 December.

The Greek Gladiators had their first encounter with Italian fighters on 8 January 1941, when a mixed formation of 21 *Mira* aircraft and PZL P.24s of 22 *Mira* intercepted an escorted IMAM Ro.37 reconnaissance biplane. At least one Gladiator, flown by Hiposminagos Antonios Papaioannou, was lost in a crash landing, its Greek pilot being badly wounded. The aeroplane, however, was claimed by the escorting G.50s of 154° *Gruppo*, which were appearing increasingly over the frontline. Strangely, the Greek fighter pilots claimed two CR.42s in this combat – perhaps they had mistaken the Ro.37 for a fighter, although it was not lost.

Adverse weather conditions, prevalent throughout most of the period, made flying impossible for the rest of January. On the 23rd of that month the RAF was reinforced by the arrival of No. 112 Sqn. The next encounters between the two biplane fighters occurred on 9 February. By then the weather had improved greatly, bringing the temperature over the Greek mountains down to polar levels. The opposing air forces were called upon to help their troops on the ground, who were heavily engaged in the area of Tepelenë, in southern Albania.

Fourteen Gladiators of No. 80 Sqn, back in the frontline after a period of rest, had taken off under the leadership of Sqn Ldr Jones, but three, including the CO, had had to turn back early. Flt Lt Pattle took over the flight, and a little later an estimated 30 to 40 CR.42s were encountered. In fact there were just 16 fighters of 150° *Gruppo*, led by Capitano Edoardo Travaglini. The Italian pilots had taken off from Vlorë at 1030 hrs to escort some bombers. At around 1200 hrs the aeroplane flown by Sergente

Birolo – a 'green' pilot just arrived from flying school – detached from the formation and started to dive gently towards the Italian lines. Fifteen minutes later Gladiators were seen, and attacked, as the *Falcos* were approaching the limit of their endurance.

When Birolo subsequently failed to return to base it was assumed that he had possibly been attacked by the Gladiators after leaving the formation, so he was posted missing. Another rookie pilot, Sottotenente Romano Maionica, who had joined the unit on 17 January, went missing in MM6938, while Travaglini, although unhurt, had to forced-land after his engine was hit. Only 12 pilots landed safely back at Vlorë at 1240 hrs, as the Fiat of Tenente Enzo Rovetta, hit in the engine during the combat, swung off the runway and struck fuel drums after it had touched down. The fighter had to be written off owing to the resulting damage, its pilot being slightly injured.

Four Gladiators were claimed shot down in return, with nine more listed as damaged. RAF pilots claimed four victories, later upgraded to seven. Gladiator N5811 was shot down, but its pilot, Flg Off F. W. Hosken, bailed out safely, and Flt Lt G. W. V. Kettlewell forced-landed N5858, the fighter having been hit in the oil radiator almost certainly by a Fiat.

Two hours later four Gladiators of 21 *Mira*, up with eight PZL P.24s of 22 and 23 *Mira*, intercepted SM.79s of 104° *Gruppo* and were in turn bounced by the escort, comprising 12 CR.42s of 160° *Gruppo* and 12 G.50s of 24° *Gruppo*. The Italian pilots, who suffered no losses, claimed one PZL and three Gladiators, brought down by Sergente Maggiore Luciano Tarantini, Sergente Aurelio Munich and Tenente Edoardo Crainz (his third Gladiator victory). The Official History of the Greek Air Force states that Gladiators L8011, piloted by Sminagos Kellas, and L7611, flown by Sminagos Demetrakopoulos, suffered structural damage. It is not known if they ever flew again. Kellas claimed two bombers and the other pilots one aircraft each.

Italian bomber raids over Ioannina on 10 February destroyed another machine of 21 *Mira* on the ground and damaged three Gladiators of No. 80 Sqn. Then, at 0750 hrs on 11 February, 17 CR.42s of 150° *Gruppo* swept in over Ioannina and strafed the airstrip. Iposminagos Kostorizos and Anthiposminagos Bardavilias had taken off at 0730 hrs and were in a tight climb at about 200m (650ft) when they were hit by the covering section of six CR.42s, led by Capitano Luigi Mariotti. They were both

Gladiator II N5829/RT-Z of No. 112 Sqn in 1940. Flying this machine, Plt Off William Vale of No. 80 Sqn claimed a Fiat G.50bis and a Fiat BR.20 over Himare, Albania, on 28 February 1941. One of the few Gladiators to survive the Greek campaign, it later served with No. 1412 (Meteorological) Flight at Khartoum, in Sudan, before being struck off charge on 1 July 1943. (Andrew Thomas)

claimed shot down. Bardavilias crashed in flames on the airfield while Kostorizos managed to evade the Fiats and land his badly damaged aeroplane in Bisdùni airstrip. Three more Gladiators were damaged on the ground during the attack.

On 13 February ace William Vale reported in his logbook that he had been shot down by an Italian fighter. This is not confirmed by his unit's ORB, but he might have been the victim of the G.50 flown by Sergente Gambetta of 154° *Gruppo*, who, mid-morning on that date, claimed a PZL over Korçë.

Activity slowed down with the failure of the last Greek offensive, and during the rest period reinforcements reached the RAF in the form of the first Hurricanes for No. 80 Sqn. No. 33 Sqn, which was already flying the Hawker fighter in Greece, also received additional examples – these aircraft were sent from Egypt. Monoplanes were increasingly appearing in Italian units too, so the biplane-versus-biplane combats now ended. The few occasions on which *Falcos* and Gladiators met up to the end of the campaign were in combats between mixed formations of monoplanes and biplanes.

The first such encounter was during the afternoon of 28 February when a large formation of Gladiators (eight from No. 80 Sqn and eleven from No. 112 Sqn) and Hurricanes (five from No. 80 Sqn and four from No. 33 Sqn) took off for an offensive patrol over the Tepelenë-Dukati area. The Hurricanes met Italian fighters and bombers and claimed many of them destroyed, including four CR.42s. The RAF biplanes then joined the fray and claimed an additional nine CR.42s and six G.50s.

When the British fighters returned to their bases it was asserted that 27 Italian aeroplanes had been shot down (the above-mentioned fighters plus eight bombers) in what had been the RAF's most successful day of the campaign. In reality the British fighters had clashed with a 15-strong formation of 160° *Gruppo*, led by Capitano Stasi, and 12 G.50s of 24° *Gruppo*, led by Tenente Colonello Eugenio Leotta, which were covering the Italian bombers arriving in the area.

The *Freccias* intercepted a formation of an estimated 'nine Spitfires' and another formation estimated at 'from 15 to 20 Glosters', claiming two Gladiators shot down confirmed and two probables. On the Italian side Capitano Ettore Foschini was wounded in the shoulder, while Tenente Mario Bellagambi had to force-land, his aircraft later being recovered. 160° *Gruppo*, after an engagement with numerous 'Glosters, Hurricanes and Spitfires coming from superior height', lost the aircraft flown by the young Sottotenente Italo Traini and had four more fighters slightly damaged, in one of which Sottotenente Raoul Francinetti was wounded. The CR.42s

Luigi Filippi in Sicily in 1941, sporting the rank of maggiore, probably while serving with 156° *Gruppo*. Filippi claimed a Gladiator over Malta on 31 July 1940, and ended the war as an ace, with seven victories – only one of these was claimed while flying the CR.42, however. (Roberto Gentilli)

also claimed two Gladiators destroyed and one probable, plus one 'Spitfire'. The only recorded RAF loss was the No. 112 Sqn Gladiator of Flt Lt R. J. Abrahams, who bailed out unhurt, probably the victim of a G.50.

Among the claims made on this day were the last ones by pilots flying No. 80 Sqn's Gladiators. During the first week in March the unit was equipped with Hurricanes and the remaining Gladiators were passed on to No. 112 Sqn.

On 13 March 14 Gladiators of No. 112 Sqn and six Hurricanes of No. 33 Sqn tangled with 11 C.200s of the newly arrived 22° *Gruppo* (which they misidentified as G.50s) and 18 CR.42s of 160° *Gruppo*. Ten *Falcos* and a G.50 were claimed for no reported losses, although heavy damage was inflicted on the aircraft of Flt Lt J. F. Fraser and Plt Off J. L. Groves. The CR.42 pilots claimed three Gladiators and one Hurricane, and an additional Gladiator was credited to the Macchis. In return, Tenente Gualtiero Bacchi and Sottotenente Enzo Torroni were killed in action.

Although the level of combat intensified during the following days, this was the last time *Falcos* and Gladiators fought each other over Greece. As a final consideration it is worth noting that Traini, Bacchi and Torroni had arrived from flying school in the middle of January, together with Sottotenente Ettore Campinoti, who was to lose his life in an aerial collision the day after this combat took place. This was a clear indication that, with the beginning of the war, the Italian training system had not kept up with operational requirements.

MALTA AND IRAQ

The legendary *Faith*, *Hope* and *Charity*, as the original Sea Gladiators defending Malta were dubbed, or, to be more precise, the six machines taken on charge by the RAF from Royal Navy stocks (N5519, N5520, N5522, N5524, N5529 and N5531) had very little occasion to meet the Sicilian-based CR.42s before being replaced by Hurricanes. In fact the only significant combat occurred on the last day of July 1940.

That morning, a single SM.79 of 109° *Gruppo* performed a photographic reconnaissance mission of Grand Harbour and the port of Marsa Scirocco, supported by a CR.42 of 23° *Gruppo* – the pilot of the latter had to make a visual reconnaissance of both targets. The two machines were covered by 12 *Falcos* of the same *gruppo*, led by Capitano Luigi Filippi. Six CR.42s had to provide a close escort for the Savoia, while the rest of the formation acted as top cover. Three Sea Gladiators were available that morning, N5519, N5520 and N5529, and they scrambled to intercept the intruders.

At 18,000ft over Valletta Flg Offs W. J. Woods, P. W. Hartley and F. F. Taylor bounced the Fiats flown by Capitano Antonio Chiodi and Sergente Manlio Tarantino, which were part of the close escort. The latter pilot was seen to dive away, followed by two of the RAF fighters, but Tarantino was able to disengage and claimed to have damaged his opponent. While the rest of the formation closed around the bomber, four fighters of the top cover, piloted by Filippi, Tenente Mario Rigatti, Maresciallo Dentis and Sergente Mantelli, dived on the Gladiators that were chasing Chiodi, and they were able to claim one shot down in flames and the other damaged. They did, however, have to witness the demise of their comrade, who fell into the sea. Filippi had shot down N5519, from which Peter Hartley was able to jump with severe burns, while Chiodi had been shot down by Woods in N5520.

Gladiators and CR.42s met on at least one other occasion, on 2 November, but only claims for probable victories were submitted, and there were no actual losses.

In 1941 CR.42s and Gladiators clashed on yet another front, this time in distant Iraq. On 1 April a military putsch in the country brought down the legitimate government and a newly-formed national defence committee decided that its first task was to do away with British forces based within Iraq. Commonwealth troops reacted almost at once, and the rebels requested the help of Italy and Germany to fight them. After a month of growing tension the British attacked on 2 May, bombing Iraqi troops gathered around the RAF airfield of Habbaniya – home to an *ad hoc* air force that had been created to support British troops fighting in Iraq. It comprised ten resident Gladiator Is plus five more Mk Is and IIs that had arrived from Egypt, led by Wg Cdr W. T. F. Wightman.

On 12 May the *Regia Aeronautica* renamed 155ª *Squadriglia* of 3° *Gruppo*, based in Sardinia, the *Squadriglia Speciale Iraq*, and ordered the unit to move forthwith to the Middle East to support the Iraqi revolt. Ten days later 12 CR.42s, specially modified with an extra fuel tank, armour protection behind the pilot's seat and Iraqi national insignia, were taken on charge by the unit, which departed on 23 May. Eleven CR.42s, led by Capitano Francesco Sforza, landed at Kirkuk on 28 May – one was left behind in Vlorë during the first leg of the journey.

The day after, following a request by the Iraqi authorities, three CR.42s flown by Tenenti Adriano Porcù and Emilio Valentini and Sergente Angelo Squarzon took off on a reconnaissance mission over Al Habbaniyah. As they neared the airfield they intercepted three Hawker Audaxes of the Habbaniyah Air Striking Force, shooting down the aircraft flown by Flt Lt Webster. The Audaxes were escorted by two Gladiators, and Wg Cdr Wightman in N5777 was able to shoot down MM7476, flown by Valentini, who was made a PoW. The other two Fiats were damaged, and back at base their pilots claimed the destruction of two Gladiators, evidently having misidentified the Audax.

On 30 May Baghdad fell into Commonwealth hands and the Iraqi revolt ended. The *Squadriglia Speciale Iraq* had to hastily flee the country, leaving behind three unserviceable Fiats. The others finally arrived in Rhodes on 4 June 1941.

STATISTICS AND ANALYSIS

The Gladiator and CR.42 clashed on relatively few occasions (44 encounters in the period up to March 1941, plus two others before year-end), so the statistical basis on which to make a comparison is quite limited. CR.42 pilots claimed some 104 victories against Gladiators while losing 51 of their number, and Gladiator pilots claimed around 138 *Falcos* while admitting the loss to their Italian opponents of only 27 fighters shot down or obliged to force- or crash-land owing to enemy action. These figures, although related to small overall numbers, give the impression that the Gloster biplane had a clear edge over its Italian opponent, with a victory-to-loss ratio of 5.1-to-1 (claimed) and of around 1.9-to-1 (real). For a comparison, studies by historian Jerry Scutts showed that the victory-to-loss ratio (real) of the Bf 109 against the Hurricane during the Battle of Britain was roughly the same.

However, studies carried out by the authors in recent years have shown that by giving full credit to the Italian sources (at least when their detailed descriptions of events match those of the RAF), and examining personal logbooks, Commonwealth pilots' recollections of events and the records of the RSUs when available, 14 more Gladiators were shot down or force-landed owing to Italian action. An additional seven were heavily damaged in combat, although it has not been possible to ascertain their ultimate fate.

Again, these are small numbers, but adding them to other known Gladiator losses definitely changes the statistics, increasing the British biplane fighter's losses to Fiat action to at least 41, and making the real victory-to-loss ratio 1.2-to-1 in favour of the Gladiator. This is more or less the same as achieved by the Bf 109 over the Spitfire during the Battle of Britain, in a match that aviation historians agree to consider even. The figure of 41 losses also tallies more closely with the total known Gladiator operational losses in Middle East Command, which is fixed at 84. The discrepancy regarding Allied losses is mainly due to the fact that the records of most Commonwealth units in the sector during this period of the conflict did not survive the war, having mainly been lost in Greece in April 1941.

Once the figures are reset, it is interesting to see how they arise from the confrontation between the two fighters. A comparative look at the two types in light of research recently conducted by Michele Maria Gaetani shows that the Fiat was definitely the best machine in respect to its performance. Although its rate-of-climb was similar to that of the Gladiator up to 3,000m (10,000ft), the CR.42 was much faster above that altitude up to 5,000m (16,000ft) owing to its smaller wing area, constant-speed propeller and the superior power of its engine, which could provide up to 960hp for short periods at emergency rating. It was in manoeuvrability that the *Falco* lost its edge, the Gladiator definitely being better in this respect.

The opposing pilots became fully aware of the respective strengths of their mounts after the first encounters, as demonstrated by the recollections of Joseph Fraser (among others):

> During July 1940 many dogfights were fought over the bay of Sollum between Gladiators and CR.42s, for the CR.42 pilot had not yet learned to respect the Gladiator – his senior – with its greater manoeuvrability.

With regard to the combat equipment of the two fighters, it is generally agreed that the Gladiator was superior to the CR.42. The Fiat fighters were designed to be equipped with two Breda SAFAT guns of 12.7mm calibre. In the years immediately before the war Breda was momentarily unable to produce enough SAFAT guns, and the last CR.32s and the first CR.42s produced had only one such weapon, backed by a smaller 7.7mm SAFAT. This mix can be considered the *Falco's* standard armament at the beginning of the war. The 12.7mm gun itself was generally praised by the pilots, who remembered its good hitting power and long range, and by the armourers, who liked its reliability. The 12.7mm Breda could also fire an effective explosive bullet, in which aluminium powder was added to the charge to increase its destructive power. After the war these factors gave this weapon an enviable reputation.

As far as effectiveness is concerned, the most relevant characteristic of an aerial gun is its ability to score hits thanks to a high rate-of-fire and a high muzzle velocity. The hitting power endowed by explosive ammunition is of lesser importance unless the target is armoured. In both of these features the Breda fell well short of the Browning 0.303-in. machine gun fitted in the Gladiator. The two SAFATs were synchronised to fire through the propeller arc, and even if the fuselage-mounted installation helped the pilots' aim, it further reduced their rate-of-fire. In respect to the latter feature, the Gladiator's Brownings (two of them also synchronised using Costantinesco fire control gear) were able to fire 2.5 times more rounds per second than the CR.42's SAFATs. This figure gives a direct measure of the superior effectiveness of these weapons if we consider that every single round of the British guns, regardless of its calibre, was potentially deadly against its unarmoured opponent.

Sgt William Vale in his personal Gladiator N5784/NW-L during the Greek campaign. Behind the cockpit access door is the prestigious coat of arms of Framlingham College, which Bill attended from the age of nine. (Brian Cull)

Like the CR.42, the Gladiator had no protection for the pilot either. Not considered necessary in Italian fighters of its era, armour had been deleted from the Gladiator for an entirely different reason. The fighting area attacks against bombers that were practised by the RAF before the war did not require back armour in fighters, as it was thought that enemy escorts were not likely to be engaged due to their modest range.

On the other hand, the need to fit all fighters with bulletproof windscreens was foreseen. In 1938 such a device was tested on Gladiator K7961, and in March 1939 it was decided that the fighter did not need to be fitted with armour plate but should have a bulletproof glass windscreen. However, it seems that this never materialised, priority being given to the monoplanes, but the first combats against the Luftwaffe showed RAF HQ that both bulletproof windscreens and back armour were needed. Again, the monoplanes took priority, and despite the fact that No. 64 Sqn called for a fully armoured Gladiator on 26 November 1939, there is no evidence that such protection was ever introduced into service. The only known armour-protected Gladiators were those of Malta's Hal Far Fighter Flight, which had their plates fitted in the field.

The Gladiator's most important advantage over the *Falco* undoubtedly lay in its radio equipment. R/T voice communication between fighters was commonly practised in the RAF before the war, and the Gladiator was no exception to this rule, being equipped with a TR 9 AM set. It did not have very long range, and the radio could be affected by vibrations and temperature changes during flight, but at least it worked.

By comparison, Italian fighters were devoid of any wireless system. Local industry had struggled to supply a complete R/T set for fighters, but in 1937 the SAFAR company developed the ARC1 (Aviation Receiver for Fighters N°1), which was officially designated to be standard equipment for all new machines. During its first trials the set proved to have serious technical defects. The receiver, for example, was both unreliable and unstable, thus requiring the pilot, who was busy flying the aircraft, to make continuous tuning adjustments. These problems soon caused most pilots to refuse to use it – an attitude worsened by their lack of specific tactical training that could have shown them the benefit of such a device, even though it was only a receiver.

Thus, in many encounters between *Falcos* and Gladiators, the TR 9 was the trump card in Allied pilots' hands. It allowed them to conduct well organised attacks and make full use of the limited number of Gladiators available when combat was joined. Thanks to good discipline in its use, the TR 9 proved to be a vital asset when it came to avoiding losses, as pilots could send timely warnings to comrades that were about to come under attack. The radio was a real force multiplier too, permitting the RAF and Commonwealth units to successfully tackle Italian formations that were very often superior in numbers but much less coordinated.

Having listed the relative strengths and weaknesses of the two machines, their performance in combat can now be summarised. The air war between CR.42s and the Gladiators can be divided into three main periods, roughly overlapping the seasons of the year. The first stage lasted from June to the end of August 1940. It saw combats over North and East Africa that demonstrated a clear superiority of the Gladiator over its opponent – 18 CR. 42s were either lost or obliged to forced-land after combat damage, compared with only 11 Gladiators.

A bare-chested pilot of No. 1 Sqn SAAF prepares to take off in Kenya. Owing to the oppressive heat, pilots sometimes chose to fly in shorts, which could have had severe consequences for them in the event of a fire. (SAAF Museum)

These numbers were influenced by two separate factors. One was the kind of engagement that took place when the biplanes confronted one another for the first time. This was, rather instinctively, the dogfight, with every pilot manoeuvring to open fire on an enemy from dead astern. Thus, the Gladiator's superior manoeuvrability was critical, enabling it to prevail in practically all the opening rounds. The other factor was that many Italian advanced landing grounds were still devoid of any anti-aircraft defence or warning network, and the RAF took full advantage of this, sending its fighters directly over these bases. Italian fighter pilots always rose to meet the challenge, suffering heavy losses in low-altitude dogfights as a result.

There were hardly any combats during September and October 1940. When they restarted, on the last day of October, the Italians, at least in Africa, had fully learned the lesson in respect to dogfighting with the Gladiator. Pilots started to use dive-and-zoom tactics instead, as they had previously done in their CR.32s over Spain in order

Flt Lt Joe Fraser of No. 112 Sqn in front of Gladiator II N5627/RT-D at Ioannina in March 1941. Fraser claimed three CR.42s in a total of six and one shared victories while flying this aircraft. He ended the war with ten kills to his name, all of them claimed while flying Gladiators – four of them were CR.42s. Gladiator N5627 probably did not survive the Greek campaign, being struck off charge on 31 May 1941. (Patricia Molloy)

One of the most successful CR.42 pilots in combat with the Gladiator was Capitano Antonio Raffi of 412ª *Squadriglia*, who claimed four of the British fighters in East Africa. (Alide Comba)

to cope with the more manoeuvrable I-15s. Three months of the most intense combats followed, with the additional front in Greece opening in November. By the end of January 1941 24 Gladiators had fallen, compared with 23 CR.42s.

The *Regia Aeronautica* had one *gruppo* commander and three *squadriglia* COs shot down during this period, the last three, two of whom were aces, being killed. The RAF and Commonwealth had three squadron leaders killed and five aces shot down, although all of the latter survived almost unhurt.

At this time clashes were highly influenced by geographical factors. Over the African fronts Fiat pilots had been able to achieve a clear margin of superiority over their opponents, obtaining 20 victories for 11 losses. However, over Greece, No. 80 Sqn had shot down 12 *Falcos* for the loss of only four of its Gladiators, thus redressing the balance. Although the British fighter's enclosed cockpit, R/T equipment and full set of blind-flying instruments could have had a greater impact in the cold winter skies of Greece, the superlative quality of the British aces of No. 80 Sqn, and of their legendary leader Thomas Pattle, is perhaps the main reason for this outstanding achievement.

It is also worth noting that from the war's outset, No. 80 Sqn had adopted a stepped formation that very much resembled that used by Fiat pilots during the Spanish Civil War. The only differences between the British and Italian formations were the smaller numbers within the No. 80 Sqn echelons and the use of R/T, which permitted greater spacing between the different levels of the formation, making it more elusive and effective.

The final period of the clashes between *Falcos* and Gladiators came in February and March 1941. The Hurricane had arrived in the ranks of most of the RAF and SAAF units by then, while the best Italian units were mostly back in Italy re-equipping with monoplanes. The intensity of the combats between biplanes diminished, ten CR.42s being lost compared with six Gladiators (one of them Greek). Seven of the missing CR.42 pilots were new arrivals fresh from flying school and one was an ace. All were killed in action.

From the Italian point of view it is surprising to see that, during the combats of this last stage of the 'biplane war', the young Fiat pilots apparently repeated the errors of the previous summer – trying to dogfight with the Gladiators, while an expert ace had again gallantly tried to take off while enemy aircraft were already orbiting overhead. This indicates that even though, over the different war fronts, units had been able to work out the best tactics to employ when up against a Gladiator in a CR.42, no lessons had filtered back to Italy to improve the training regime for new pilots in the fighter schools, or to standardise the teaching of better tactics in these establishments.

Gladiator Aces with CR.42 Claims

Name	Unit	CR.42 claims	Total Gladiator Score/Overall Score
Plt Off Richard Acworth	No. 112 Sqn	2	4/7
Flg Off Wilfred Arthur	No. 3 Sqn RAAF	2	2/8
Flg Off Alan Boyd	No. 3 Sqn RAAF	6	6/6
Capt Brian Boyle	No. 1 Sqn SAAF	3	3/5
Flt Lt George Burges	No. 261 Sqn	1	3/7
Sgt Charles Casbolt	No. 80 Sqn	4	5/13
Flg Off Homer Cochrane	No. 112 Sqn	4	7/7
Flt Sgt Leonard Cottingham	No. 33 Sqn	3	4/11
Flt Lt Nigel Cullen	No. 80 Sqn	2	6/16
Flg Off Ernest Dean	No. 33 Sqn	1	2/5
Sgt George Donaldson	No. 112 Sqn	1	6/6
Sqn Ldr Patrick Dunn	No. 80 Sqn	2	2/6
Flt Lt Joseph Fraser	No. 112 Sqn	4	10/10
Flt Lt Charles Fry	No. 112 Sqn	1	4/5
Sgt Donald Gregory	No. 80 Sqn	8	8/8
Plt Off Jack Groves	No. 112 Sqn	3	4/6
Sgt Edward Hewett	No. 80 Sqn	2	3/16
Lt John Hewitson	No. 1 Sqn SAAF	1 sh.	1/5
Sqn Ldr Edward Jones	No. 80 Sqn	5	5/5
Flt Lt George Kettlewell	No. 80 Sqn	2	3/5
Flg Off Sidney Linnard	No. 80 Sqn	2	2/6
Lt Robin Pare	No. 1 Sqn SAAF	1	2/6
Flt Lt Thomas Pattle	No. 80 Sqn	10	15/50+
Flt Lt Lloyd Schwab	No. 112 Sqn	2	6/6
Flt Lt Gordon Steege	No. 3 Sqn RAAF	2	3/8
Flg Off Vincent Stuckey	No. 80 Sqn	3	5/5
Plt Off William Vale	No. 80 Sqn	6	10/30
Plt Off Peter Wickham	Att. No. 33 Sqn	1	4/10
Flg Off William Woods	Hal Far Fighter Flight	1	2/6
Plt Off Vernon Woodward	No. 33 Sqn	2	4/18
Flg Off Peter Wykeham-Barnes	No. 80 Sqn	1	3/14

CR.42 Aces with Gladiator Claims			
Name	Unit(s)	Gladiator claims	Total CR.42 Score/ Total Score
Cap Paolo Arcangeletti	393ª Sq.	1	2/5
Serg Magg Luigi Baron	412ª Sq.	4	12/12
Serg Alessandro Bladelli	91ª Sq.	1 sh.	5 sh./5
Cap Guido Bobba	74ª Sq.	1	4/5
Ten Pietro Bonfatti	73ª Sq.	1	2/6
Magg Ernesto Botto	9° Gr.	1 sh.	3/8
Ten Guglielmo Chiarini	82ª Sq.	1	5/5
M.llo Rinaldo Damiani	97ª Sq.	1 sh.	3 sh./6
Cap Luigi Filippi	75ª Sq.	1	1/7
Sottoten Jacopo Frigerio	97ª Sq.	1 sh.	3 sh./5
Ten Eber Giudici	393ª Sq.	1	1/5
Cap Antonio Larsimont Pergameni	97ª Sq. & 9° Gr.	1	1/7
Ten Franco Lucchini	90ª Sq.	2	3/22
Cap Luigi Mariotti	363ª Sq.	1	1/5
Serg Teresio Martinoli	78ª Sq.	1	3/22
Serg Elio Miotto	91ª Sq.	3 sh.	8 sh./5
Cap Luigi Monti	91ª Sq. & 84ª Sq.	5 sh.	19 sh./8
Ten Giuseppe Oblach	73ª Sq.	1	1/7
Serg Luciano Perdoni	84ª Sq.	2 sh.	2 sh./5
Sottoten Alvaro Querci	73ª Sq.	2 sh.	2 sh./6
Cap Antonio Raffi	412ª Sq.	4	4/5
Serg Magg Angelo Savini	90ª Sq.	3 sh.	5 sh./7
Ten Claudio Solaro	70ª Sq.	1 sh.	1/12
Ten Alberto Spigaglia	364ª Sq.	1	1/6
Ten Giulio Torresi	77ª Sq.	2	6/10
Serg Mario Veronesi	84ª Sq.	2 sh.	2/11
Cap Ezio Viglione Borghese	97ª Sq. & 96ª Sq.	1	1/5

AFTERMATH

The Gloster Gladiator and Fiat CR.42 fought each other from 19 June 1940 to the end of the Greek Campaign, as well as during the British Offensive in Eritrea. Two odd encounters took place in May and October 1941, when the Gladiator and the CR.42 were no longer the principal fighters of their countries in any sector, and indeed the Gladiator had all but disappeared from frontline service. As far as the direct confrontation between the two types is concerned, the outcome of these nine months of air war, which led to the brilliant victories of Sir Archibald Wavell's armies in North and East Africa, was an even match.

The encounters between the two types were relatively few, as a direct result of the conservative employment of their forces by the *Regia Aeronautica* and RAF in the opening stages of the war. For RAF Middle East Command, this policy of non-aggression was a way to save precious resources until reinforcement in the form of more modern fighters and bombers could be flown in from the UK to start the offensive. For the *Regia Aeronautica*, such a tactic was the only choice available to it, as Italian industry and flying schools could not keep pace with the losses imposed by a prolonged war effort – the nation's entry into the war had been based upon the assumption that it would be a short-lived conflict.

Bearing the foregoing in mind, both types accomplished their task of bridging the gap until monoplanes were deployed, with neither one being able to overwhelm its opponent. Occasional successes were obtained on both fronts. At the beginning of July 1940 the Gladiators of No. 94 Sqn were critical in forcing the *Regia Aeronautica* to leave its base at Assab, which was potentially very dangerous for Commonwealth forces in Aden.

In August of that year the *Regia Aeronautica's* Fiats swept the skies of British Somaliland during the Italian invasion, and in September the timidly advancing army of Marshal Graziani in Libya was covered from dawn to dusk by swarms of CR.42s that prevented any form of RAF daylight intervention. Finally, at the beginning of November, the first Commonwealth land offensive of the war against Metemma and Gallabat was repulsed by the Italians with the fundamental help of the air force after the *Falcos* had swept the sky clear of their opponent's fighters. These were, however, small local actions that had very little impact on the trend of the war.

After the fall of Greece the Gladiator practically disappeared from frontline service, but the CR.42 soldiered on until war's end. It cannot be denied that the presence of a biplane over the battlefields in 1942-43 was somewhat anachronistic, and a result of the backwardness of the Italian industrial system, but it should not be forgotten that the *Falco* continued to show a certain level of effectiveness. In 1940 the aircraft had been quite effective in the important role of bomber interceptor, opposing Blenheims, Wellesleys, Battles and Wellingtons, and shooting down a hundred of them for minimal losses.

The Gladiator, whose characteristics were optimised for dogfighting, had on the contrary proved painfully inadequate when put up against fast Italian bombers, being able to shoot down only a handful of them, and suffering almost as many losses in the process. In the authors' opinion this was the main reason for the Gladiator's quick retirement from the frontline, despite the very good results obtained against enemy fighters.

With its days as a fighter at an end, the *Falco* went on to serve in the point-defence or convoy-escort roles, continuing to shoot down a number of enemy aircraft well into the autumn of 1941. The arrival of new American medium and heavy bombers in 1942 marked the end of its residual capacity as a daylight interceptor, but the type was still able to find new roles as a fighter-bomber and nightfighter until Italy's surrender in September 1943 – a show of versatility that had no equal, at least in the ranks of the *Regia Aeronautica*.

FURTHER READING

SELECT BIBLIOGRAPHY

Brioschi, Angelo, *Ali e Colori no. 1 Fiat CR 42* (La Bancarella Aeronautica, 1999)

Cull, Brian, with Minterne, Don, *Hurricanes over Tobruk* (Grub Street, 1999)

Cull, Brian, with Slongo, Ludovico and Gustavsson, Håkan, *Gladiator Ace – Bill 'Cherry' Vale, the RAF's Forgotten Fighter Ace* (Haynes, 2010)

Cull, Brian, Galea Frederick, *Gladiators over Malta – The story of Faith, Hope and Charity* (Wise Owl, 2008)

Garello, Giancarlo, 'Les ailes Italiennes en Iraq' (1937-1941), *Avions* No 184, November-December 2011

Gustavsson, Håkan, and Slongo, Ludovico, *Desert Prelude – Early Clashes* (MMP, 2010)

Gustavsson, Håkan, and Slongo, Ludovico, *Desert Prelude – 'Operation Compass'* (MMP, 2011)

Gustavsson, Håkan, and Slongo, Ludovico, *Osprey Aircraft of the Aces 90 - Fiat CR.42 Aces of World War 2* (Osprey, 2009)

Mason, Francis K., *The Gloster Gladiator* (MacDonald, 1964)

Napier, Sid, 'The Hellenic Gladiators', *Small Air Forces Observer* Vol 27 No 4, April 2005

Shores, Christopher, *Dust Clouds in the Middle East* (Grub Street, 1996)

Shores, Christopher, and Cull, Brian, with Nicola Malizia, *Air War for Yugoslavia, Greece and Crete 1940-41* (Grub Street, 1987)

Shores, Christopher, and Cull, Brian, with Nicola Malizia, *Malta: The Hurricane Years 1940-41* (Grub Street, 1987)

Shores, Christopher, and Ricci, Corrado, *la Guerra Aerea in Africa Orientale 1940-41* (Mucchi, 1980)

Thomas, Andrew, *Osprey Aircraft of the Aces 44 - Gloster Gladiator Aces* (Osprey, 2002)

INDEX

References to illustrations are shown in **bold**.